THE CLASS SIZE
DEBATE

Other books from the Economic Policy Institute

The State of Working America

Market-Based Reforms in Urban Education

School Vouchers:
Examining the Evidence

Can Public Schools Learn From Private Schools?

Where's the Money Gone?
Changes in the Level and Composition of Education Spending

Risky Business:
Private Management of Public Schools

School Choice:
Examining the Evidence

THE CLASS SIZE DEBATE

◆

Lawrence Mishel & Richard Rothstein, editors

Alan B. Krueger, Eric A. Hanushek,
& Jennifer King Rice, contributors

ECONOMIC POLICY INSTITUTE

Washington, D.C.

The Class Size Debate is a publication of
the Economic Policy Institute's Education Program.

ECONOMIC POLICY INSTITUTE
1660 L Street, NW, Suite 1200
Washington, D.C. 20036

http://www.epinet.org

ISBN: 0-944826-92-X

Table of contents

About the editors & contributors

Lawrence Mishel is the vice president of the Economic Policy Institute and was its research director from 1987 to 1999. His areas of research are labor economics, wage and income distribution, industrial relations, productivity growth, and the economics of education. He is the co-author (with Jared Bernstein and Heather Boushey) of the forthcoming *State of Working America 2002-03* and the co-editor of *Beware the U.S. Model* (with John Schmitt) and *Unions and Economic Competitiveness* (with Paula Voos). He holds a Ph.D. in economics from the University of Wisconsin.

Richard Rothstein is a research associate of the Economic Policy Institute, the national education columnist for *The New York Times,* a contributing editor of *The American Prospect,* and an adjunct professor of public policy at Occidental College in Los Angeles. He is the author of *Can Public Schools Learn From Private Schools?* (with Martin Carnoy and Richard Benveniste); *The Way We Were? The Myths and Realities of America's Student Achievement*; and *Where's the Money Gone? Changes in the Level and Composition of Education Spending 1967-91*; and co-editor (with Edith Rasell) of *School Choice: Examining the Evidence.*

Alan B. Krueger is the Bendheim Professor of Economics and Public Affairs at Princeton University. Since 1987 he has held a joint appointment in the Economics Department and Woodrow Wilson School at Princeton. He has published articles in academic journals on a wide range of subjects, including unemployment, social insurance, labor demand, the economics of education, income dispersion, technological change, health economics, and environmental economics. He is author of *Education Matters: Selected Essays on Education by Alan B. Krueger,* co-editor (with Robert Solow) of *The Roaring Nineties: Can Full Employment Be Sustained?* and, since 1996, editor of the *Journal of Economic Perspectives*, a journal of the American Economic Association. In 1994-95 he served as chief economist of the U.S. Department of Labor. He received a Ph.D. in economics from Harvard University in 1987.

Eric A. Hanushek is the Paul and Jean Hanna Senior Fellow at the Hoover Institution of Stanford University and a research associate of the National Bureau of Economic Research. He is a leading expert on educational policy with an emphasis on the economics and finance of schools. His books include *Improving America's Schools, Making Schools Work, Educational Performance of the Poor, Education and Race, Assessing Policies for Retirement Income,*

Modern Political Economy, Improving Information for Social Policy Decisions, and *Statistical Methods for Social Scientists*, along with numerous articles in professional journals. He has held a number of posts in government, including deputy director of the Congressional Budget Office, senior staff economist at the Council of Economic Advisers, and senior economist at the Cost of Living Council. He earned a Ph.D. in economics at the Massachusetts Institute of Technology.

Jennifer King Rice is an assistant professor in the Department of Education Policy and Leadership at the University of Maryland. Her research interests include education policy, education productivity, cost analysis applications to education, and educational reforms for at-risk students. Her publications and presentations have precipitated invitations to share her expertise with various organizations including the U.S. Department of Education, the Maryland State Department of Education, the New York State Board of Regents, the Maryland State Attorney General's Office, the National Center for Education Statistics, and the Society of Government Economists. She earned a Ph.D. from Cornell University.

Acknowledgments

Prof. Krueger's paper is a revised and extended version of a paper that was originally prepared for a conference sponsored by Temple University's Center for Research in Human Development and Education, titled, "What Do We Know About How to Make Small Classes Work?" held December 6-7, 1999 in Washington, D.C. The paper was written while Prof. Krueger was on leave at the Center for Advanced Study in the Behavioral Sciences at Stanford University. He is grateful to Diane Whitmore and Michael Watts for excellent research assistance, to Victor Fuchs for helpful comments, and to Eric Hanushek for providing the data used in Section I. Jesse Rothstein provided valuable editorial assistance. The Center for Advanced Study in the Behavioral Sciences, Temple's Center for Research in Human Development and Education, and Princeton's Industrial Relations Section provided financial support.

Helpful comments on Prof. Hanushek's paper were provided by John Kain, Steve Landsburg, Ed Lazear, Terry Moe, Paul Peterson, Macke Raymond, and Steve Rivkin.

Introduction

For three decades, a belief that public education is wasteful and inefficient has played an important role in debates about its reform. Those who have proposed new spending programs for schools to improve student achievement have been on the defensive. The presumption has been that changes in structure and governance of schools — like choice, vouchers, charter schools, standards, accountability, and assessment — are the only way to improve student outcomes. Traditional interventions, like smaller class size and higher teacher salaries, have been presumed ineffective.

Voters and state and local political leaders have never been as impressed with this statement of alternatives as have national policy makers and scholars. Throughout the last third of the 20th century, when the idea that "money makes no difference" held sway in academic circles, spending in public education increased at a steady rate, and class sizes declined. But, as we showed in a 1995 Economic Policy Institute report, *Where's the Money Gone?*, the spending has increased more slowly than most people believe. It can't be known whether the rate would have been more rapid in the absence of an academic consensus regarding public education's inefficiency.

The leading proponent of the prevailing view that money doesn't make a difference has been Eric A. Hanushek, now of the Hoover Institution. Dr. Hanushek has played two roles. As a scholar, he has conducted a series of influential literature reviews that support the conclusion that increased spending in general, and smaller class size in particular, do not "systematically" lead to improved student achievement. There have been hundreds of research studies that attempt to assess the relationship of spending and achievement. Dr. Hanushek has found that, in some cases, the relationship is positive, but in others no positive relationship can be discerned, either because the relationship is negative or because it is statistically insignificant.

These findings have led Dr. Hanushek to play another role — as a very visible public advocate for restraining the growth of spending in public schools. He chaired a task force of the Brookings Institution, leading to the publication of *Making Schools Work: Improving Performance and Con-*

1

trolling Costs, a very influential 1993 book that asserts, "Despite ever rising school budgets, student performance has stagnated....[I]n recent years the costs of education have been growing far more quickly than the benefits." Dr. Hanushek has testified in many state court cases regarding the equity and adequacy of school spending, generally in support of the proposition that increased funds are not a likely source of improved student achievement. He is also frequently cited in newspapers and magazines in support of this proposition.

Dr. Hanushek's academic research, inventorying and summarizing existing studies of the relationship between spending and achievement, does not inexorably lead to conclusions about the desirability of restraining school spending. Even if his conclusion about the lack of a "systematic" relationship is unchallenged, it remains the case that some studies show a positive relationship, and therefore it might be possible to determine when, and under what conditions, higher spending produces student achievement. Dr. Hanushek states as much in almost all of his academic publications, but with the caveat that "simply knowing that some districts might use resources effectively does not provide any guide to effective policy, unless many more details can be supplied." However, Dr. Hanushek's research has not led a generation of scholars and policy makers to seek to supply these details. Rather, the impact has mostly been to encourage policy makers to look away from resource solutions and toward structural and governance changes.

In recent years, the most important challenge to this dominant trend has arisen because of an unusual experiment (STAR, or the Student Teacher Achievement Ratio study) conducted by the state of Tennessee. Attempting to determine whether achievement would increase with smaller class sizes, the state legislature authorized schools to volunteer to participate in an experiment whereby they would receive additional funds for lower class sizes for kindergarten to third-grade classes, provided that students and teachers were randomly assigned to regular (large) or small classes.

The result was significantly enhanced achievement for children, especially minority children, in smaller classes. This single study persuaded many scholars and policy makers that smaller classes do make a difference, because the study was believed to be of so much higher quality than the hundreds of non-experimental studies about which Dr. Hanushek had relied for his summaries. Most theoreticians have long believed that conducting true randomized field experiments is the only valid method for resolving disputes of this kind. The reason is that, in non-experimental studies, comparisons between groups must ultimately rely on researchers' assumptions about similarity of the groups' characteristics. This makes the studies subject to errors from mis-specification (for example, assuming that black students who receive free or reduced-price lunch subsidies are similar in relevant respects to white students who receive these subsidies) or from omitted variables (for example, failing to recognize that parental education levels are important determinants of student achievement).

Randomized field trials, on the other hand, avoid these flaws because, if treatment and control groups are randomly selected from large enough populations, researchers can assume that their relevant characteristics (whatever those characteristics may be) will be equally distributed between the two groups. In a non-experimental study, retrospective comparison of student achievement in small and large classes may lead to the conclusion that small classes are superior only because of some unobserved characteristic that distinguishes the two groups, besides the size of their classes. In an experimental study, results are more reliable because the unobserved characteristics, whatever they may be, are evenly distributed.

It is hard to avoid the conclusion that however valid the Tennessee study will ultimately be judged to have been, enthusiasm for it has been somewhat excessive because another principle of scientific experimentation is that results should be confirmed over and over again before acceptance, in different laboratories where unobserved laboratory conditions may be different. In this case, even if the Tennessee results are entirely reliable, policy conclusions are being drawn that go beyond what the Tennessee results can support. For example, the Tennessee study showed that small classes are superior to large ones, but because both types of classes were mostly taught by teachers trained in Tennessee colleges, earning similar salaries on average, it is possible that the results would not be reproduced by teachers trained in different institutions, having different qualifications, or earning higher or lower salaries. As another example, the Tennessee study found that student achievement was higher in classes of about 16 than in classes of about 24. The Tennessee study itself cannot suggest whether other degrees of reductions in class size would also boost achievement.

Nonetheless, the Tennessee study has had great influence on policy makers. In California, the governor and legislature made the needed additional money available to all schools that reduced class sizes to 20 in grades K-3. California previously had nearly the largest class sizes in the nation, so the reductions were substantial. But implementation of this policy illustrates the dangers of rushing to make policy changes based on limited research. Because California increased its demand for elementary school teachers so suddenly, many teachers without training or credentials were hired. At the same time, many experienced teachers, working in lower-income and minority communities, transferred to districts with more affluent and easier-to-teach students, taking advantage of the vast numbers of sudden openings in suburban districts. Class size reduction therefore had the result in California of reducing the average experience (and, presumably quality) of K-3 teachers in the inner city. Nonetheless, since the implementation of the class size reduction policy, test scores in California schools, including schools that are heavily minority and low income, rose. But because California simultaneously implemented other policy changes (abolition of bilingual education, a stronger accountability system), it is uncertain to what extent class size reduction has been responsible for the test score gains.

Thus, as we enter a new decade, these two controversial lines of research — Dr. Hanushek's conclusion that there is no systematic relationship between resources and achievement, and the STAR results that smaller class sizes do make a difference — while not entirely inconsistent, are contending for public influence.

In the following pages, the Economic Policy Institute presents a new critique of Dr. Hanushek's methodology by Alan Krueger, a professor of economics at Princeton, and a reply by Dr. Hanushek.

Dr. Krueger's paper has two parts. First, he criticizes Dr. Hanushek's "vote counting" method, or how Dr. Hanushek adds together previous studies that find a positive relationship and those that find none. In particular, Dr. Krueger notes that many of the published studies on which Dr. Hanushek's conclusions rely contain multiple estimates of the relationship between resources and achievement, and in particular between pupil-teacher ratio and achievement. In these cases, Dr. Hanushek counted each estimate separately to arrive at the overall total of studies that suggested either a positive, negative, or statistically insignificant effect for resources. But Dr. Krueger suggests that it would be more appropriate to count each publication as a single "study," rather than counting separately each estimate within a publication. By counting each publication as only one result, Dr. Krueger concludes that the effect of resources on achievement is much more positive than Dr. Hanushek found.

In the second part of his paper, Dr. Krueger applies the findings of the Tennessee STAR experiment to his own previous research on the effect of school spending on the subsequent earnings of adults, and to similar research conducted with British data. From assumptions about future interest rates, Dr. Krueger estimates the long-term economic benefits in greater income from class size reduction, and concludes that, with plausible assumptions, the benefits can be substantial, exceeding the costs.

In this respect, Dr. Krueger's paper is an important advance in debates about education productivity. By comparing the long-term economic benefits and costs of a specific intervention, he has shown that education policy making can go beyond an attempt to evaluate school input policies solely by short-term test score effects. While, in this preliminary exploration, Dr. Krueger has had to make substantial assumptions about the organization and financial structures of schools (assumptions he notes in "caveats" in the paper), he has defined a framework for the cost-benefit analysis of school spending for other researchers to explore, elaborate, and correct.[1]

Dr. Hanushek responds to each of the Krueger analyses. With regard to the claim that "vote counting" should be based on only one "vote" per published study, Dr. Hanushek challenges the statistical assumptions behind Dr. Krueger's view and concludes, again, that his own method, of counting each estimate as a separate study, is more valid. Dr. Krueger's method, he suspects, was designed mainly for the purpose of getting a more positive result.

With respect to Dr. Krueger's estimates of the long-term economic effects of class size reduction, Dr. Hanushek notes that the estimates ultimately rely solely on evidence of labor market experiences of young Britons in the 1980s. "While it may be academically interesting to see if there is any plausibility to the kinds of class size policies being discussed, one would clearly not want to commit the billions of dollars implied by the policies on the basis of these back-of-the-envelope calculations."

It is unfortunate that the subject of public education has become so polarized that policy debates, allegedly based on scholarly research, have become more contentious than the research itself seems to require. A careful reading of the papers that follow cannot fail to lead readers to the conclusion that there is substantial agreement between these antagonists. It is perhaps best expressed by Dr. Hanushek when he states,

> Surely class size reductions are beneficial in specific circumstances — for specific groups of students, subject matters, and teachers....Second, class size reductions necessarily involve hiring more teachers, and teacher quality is much more important than class size in affecting student outcomes. Third, class size reduction is very expensive, and little or no consideration is given to alternative and more productive uses of those resources.

Similarly, in his paper, Dr. Krueger states,

> The effect sizes found in the STAR experiment and much of the literature are greater for minority and disadvantaged students than for other students. Although the critical effect size differs across groups with different average earnings, economic considerations suggest that resources would be optimally allocated if they were targeted toward those who benefit the most from smaller classes.

It is difficult to imagine that Dr. Krueger would disagree with Dr. Hanushek's statement, or that Dr. Hanushek would disagree with Dr. Krueger's.

Too often, scholarship in education debates is converted into simplified and dangerous soundbites. Sometimes liberals, particularly in state-level controversies about the level, equity, or adequacy of per-pupil spending, seem to permit themselves to be interpreted as claiming that simply giving more money to public schools, without any consideration to how that money will be spent, is a proven effective strategy. In contrast, conservatives sometimes permit themselves to be interpreted as claiming that money makes no difference whatsoever, and that schools with relatively few resources can improve sufficiently simply by being held accountable for results.

But surely the debate should not be so polarized. All should be able to agree that some schools have spent their funds effectively, and others have not. All should be able to agree that targeting the expenditure of new funds in ways that have proven to be effective is far preferable to "throwing money at schools" without regard to how it will be spent. All should be able to agree that there is strong reason to suspect that minority and disadvantaged children can benefit more than others from a combination of smaller class sizes and more effective teachers. And all should be able to agree that much more research is needed to understand precisely what the most effective expenditures on schools and other social institutions might be if improving student achievement, and narrowing the gap in achievement between advantaged and disadvantaged children are the goals.

It is difficult to avoid the conclusion that continued debates about whether money in the abstract makes a difference in education, without specifying how it might be spent, are unproductive. Equally true, denying that specific resource enhancements, alongside policy changes, can be an essential part of any reform agenda is also unproductive. Hopefully, the Krueger-Hanushek dialogue that follows can help to focus future debates on where spending is more effective. And it can add a new dimension to these debates, by proposing a comparison of the longer-term economic benefits of school spending, compared to its costs, that has barely begun to be explored.

Endnote

1. Indeed, other researchers are starting to examine both the costs and the benefits of policy interventions such as lower class size. Doug Harris (2002) uses a simulation model to estimate the "optimal" use of resources, considering teacher salaries and class size. Other researchers have examined the return on class size relative to other interventions.

CHAPTER 1

Understanding the magnitude and effect of class size on student achievement

Alan B. Krueger

At heart, questions concerning the desirability of spending more money to reduce class size involve economics, the study of how scarce resources are allocated to produce goods and services to satisfy society's competing desires. Aside from the opportunity cost of students' time, teachers are the most important, and most costly, factor of production in education. The "education production function" — that is, the relationship between schooling inputs, such as teachers per student, and schooling outputs, such as student achievement — is a special case of production functions more generally. As in other service industries, output in the education sector is hard to measure. In practice, educational output is most commonly measured by student performance on standardized tests, which is an incomplete measure for many reasons, not least because test scores are only weakly related to students' subsequent economic outcomes. Nonetheless, the output of the education sector is particularly important for the economy as a whole because as much as 70% of national income can be attributed to "human capital."[1] The education production function is thus central to understanding the economy, just as economics is central to understanding the education production function.

In recent years, a number of researchers and commentators have argued that the education production function is broken. Most prominently, in a series of influential literature summaries, Eric Hanushek (1986, 1989, 1996a, 1996b, 1997, 1998b) concludes that, "There is no strong or consistent relationship between school inputs and student performance."[2] Although Hanushek never defines his criterion for a strong or consistent relationship, he apparently draws this conclusion from his findings that "studies" are almost equally likely to find negative effects of small class sizes on achievement as they are to find positive effects, and that a majority of the estimates in the literature are statistically insignificant.[3] A number of other authors have consequently concluded that the presumed failure of the education system to convert inputs into measurable outputs is an indication that incentives in public education are incapable of producing desired results. For example, John Chubb and Terry Moe (1990) argue that the "existing [educational] institutions cannot solve the problem, because they are the problem." And Chester Finn (1991) writes, "If you were setting out to devise an organization in which nobody was in command and in which, therefore, no one could easily be held accountable for results, you would come up with a structure much like American public education." In short, these critics argue that bureaucracy, unions, and perverse incentives cause public education to squander resources, severing the link between school inputs and outputs. Many observers have concluded from these arguments that it would be wasteful to put additional resources into the current public education system — either to make the system more equitable or to increase resources for all students — because they would have no effect on educational outcomes.

Hanushek's literature reviews have had widespread influence on the allocation of school resources. He has testified about his literature summaries in school financing cases in Alabama, California, Missouri, New Hampshire, New York, Maryland, New Jersey, and Tennessee, and in several congressional hearings, and his tabulations summarizing the literature have been widely cited by expert witnesses in other venues. Moreover, the presumed absence of a relationship between resources and student outcomes for the average school district has led many to support a switch to school vouchers, or a system that penalizes schools with low-achieving students. However, a reanalysis of Hanushek's literature reviews, detailed in Section I below, shows that his results depend crucially on the peculiar way in which he combines the many studies in the literature. Specifically, Hanushek places more weight on studies from which he extracted more estimates.

Hanushek's (1997) latest published summary of the literature on class size is based on 277 estimates drawn from 59 studies. Considerably more estimates were extracted from some studies than from others. Although the distinction between estimates and studies is often blurred, Hanushek's analysis applies equal weight to every estimate, and therefore assigns much more weight to some studies than others.[4] Hanushek's pessimistic conclusion about the performance of the education production function results in part from the fact that he inadvertently places disproportionate weight on studies that are based on smaller samples. This pattern arises because Hanushek used a selection rule that would take more estimates from studies that analyzed subsamples of a larger dataset than from studies that used the full sample of the larger dataset.

For example, if one study analyzed a pooled sample of third through sixth graders, it would generate a single estimate, whereas if another study using *the same data* analyzed separate subsamples of third graders, fourth graders, fifth graders, and sixth graders, that study would generate four estimates. Moreover, if the second study estimated separate models for black, white, and Hispanic students it would yield 12 estimates by Hanushek's selection rule. And if the study further estimated separate regressions for math and reading scores for each subsample, as opposed to the average test score, it would yield 24 estimates. As a consequence of this selection rule, the lion's share of Hanushek's 277 estimates were extracted from a small minority of the 59 studies. Specifically, 44% of the estimates come from a mere 15% of the studies. Many of these estimates are based on small subsamples of larger datasets, and are therefore very imprecise.[5] Other things being equal, estimates based on smaller samples are likely to yield weaker and less systematic results. Thus, in the example above, the 24 estimates from the second study would be considerably less precise, and therefore less likely to be statistically significant, than the single estimate from the first study; nevertheless, in Hanushek's weighting scheme the second study is given an effective weight 24 times as large as the first study.

When the various studies in Hanushek's sample are accorded equal weight, *class size is systematically related to student performance,* even using Hanushek's classification of the estimates — which in some cases appears to be problematic.

A more general point raised by the reanalysis of Hanushek's literature summary is that not all estimates are created equal. One should take more seriously those estimates that use larger samples, better data, and appropriate statistical techniques to identify the effects of class size reduction. Hedges, Laine, and Greenwald (1994) and other formal meta-analyses of class size effects reach a different conclusion than Hanushek largely because they combine estimates across studies in a way that takes account of the estimates' precision. Although their approach avoids the statistical pitfalls generated by Hanushek's method, it will still yield uninformative results if the equations underlying the studies in the literature are misspecified. Research is not democratic. In any field, one good study can be worth more than the rest of the literature. There is no substitute for understanding the specifications underlying the literature and conducting well-designed experiments.

largest and best-designed experiment in the class size literature is Tennessee's Project STAR (Student/Teacher Achievement Ratio). According to the Harvard statistician Frederick Mosteller (1995), Project STAR "is one of the most important educational investigations ever carried out and illustrates the kind and magnitude of research needed in the field of education to strengthen schools." Studies based on the STAR experiment find that class size has a significant effect on test scores: reducing class size from 22 to 15 in the early primary grades seems to increase both math and reading test scores by about 0.2 standard deviations (see, e.g., Finn and Achilles 1990 or Krueger 1999b). One could argue that the careful design of the STAR experiment makes these results more persuasive than the rest of the literature on class size.

Section II below considers the economic implications of the magnitude of the relationship between class size and student performance. Reducing class sizes is expensive, and it is reasonable to ask whether the benefits justify the cost. Most of the literature on class size reduction tests whether one can statistically reject the hypothesis of zero effect on performance. But for most purposes a zero effect is not a meaningful null hypothesis to test. A more appropriate question is, "How big an improvement in student performance is necessary to justify the cost?" This question is tackled here, and a provisional answer to it is then compared to the benefits from smaller classes found by the STAR experiment. The calculations described in Section II, subject to the many caveats listed there, suggest that the economic benefits of further reductions in class size in grades K-3 are at least equal to the costs.

While it is possible that a change in incentives and enhanced competition among schools could improve the efficiency of public schools, such a conclusion should rest on direct evidence that private schools are more efficacious than public schools, or on evidence that competition improves performance, not on a presumption that public schools as currently constituted fail to transform inputs into outputs. Before profound changes in schools are made because of a presumed — and apparently inaccurate — conclusion that resources are unrelated to achievement, compelling evidence of the efficacy of the proposed changes should be required.

I. Reanalysis of Hanushek's literature review

To enable this reanalysis, Eric Hanushek provided the classification of estimates and studies underlying his 1997 literature summary.[6] As he writes (1997, 142),

> This summary concentrates on a set of published results available through 1994, updating and extending previous summaries (Hanushek 1981,

TABLE 1-1   Distribution of class size studies and estimates taken in Hanushek (1997)

Number of estimates used (1)	Number of studies (2)	Number of estimates contributed (3)	Percent of studies (4)	Percent of estimates (5)
1	17	17	28.8%	6.1%
2-3	13	28	22.0	10.1
4-7	20	109	33.9	39.4
8-24	9	123	15.3	44.4
Total	59	277	100.0	100.0

Note: Column (1) categorizes the studies according to the number of estimates that were taken from the study. Column (2) reports the number of studies that fall into each category. Column (3) reports the total number of estimates contributed from the studies. Column (4) reports the number of studies in the category as a percent of the total number of studies. Column (5) reports the number of studies in the category as a percent of the total number of estimates used from all the studies.

1986, 1989). The basic studies meet minimal criteria for analytical design and reporting of results. Specifically, the studies must be published in a book or journal (to ensure a minimal quality standard), must include some measures of family background in addition to at least one measure of resources devoted to schools, and must provide information about statistical reliability of the estimates of how resources affect student performance.

Hanushek describes his rule for selecting estimates from the various studies in the literature as follows:

The summary relies on all of the separate estimates of the effects of resources on student performance. For tabulation purposes, a "study" is a separate estimate of an educational production found in the literature. Individual published analyses typically contain more than one set of estimates, distinguished by different measures of student performance, by different grade levels, and frequently by entirely different sampling designs.

Most of the studies underlying Hanushek's literature summary were published in economics journals.

Table 1-1 summarizes the distribution of the estimates and studies underlying Hanushek's literature tabulation. The first column reports the number of estimates used from each study, dividing studies into those where only one estimate was used (first row), two or three were used (second row), four to seven were used (third row), or eight or more were used (fourth row). Seventeen studies contributed only one estimate each,[7] while nine studies contributed eight or more estimates each. These latter nine studies made up only 15% of the total set of studies, yet they contributed 44% of all estimates used. By contrast, the 17 studies from which only one estimate was taken represented 29% of studies in the literature and only 6% of the estimates.

A consideration of Hanushek's classification of some of the individual studies in the literature helps to clarify his procedures. Two studies by Link and Mulligan (1986 and 1991) each contributed 24 estimates, or 17% of all estimates. Both papers estimated separate models for math and reading scores by grade level (third, fourth, fifth, or sixth) and by race (black, white, or Hispanic), yielding 2 x 4 x 3 = 24 estimates apiece. One of these papers (Link and Mulligan 1986) addressed the merits of a longer school day by using an 8% subsample of the dataset used in the other paper (1991). Class size was not the focus of this paper, and it was included in the regression specifications only in an interaction with peer ability levels. In a passing statement, Link and Mulligan (1986, 376) note that, when they included class size separately in their 12 equations for the math score, the result was individually statistically insignificant.[8] Link and Mulligan (1991), which concentrated on estimating the impact of peer group effects on student achievement, did not explicitly control for family background in any of its estimates, although separate equations were estimated for black, white, and Hispanic students.

By contrast, Card and Krueger (1992a) focused on ⁻the effect of school resources on the payoff from attending school longer, and presented scores of estimates for 1970 and 1980 Census samples of white males sometimes exceeding one million observations (see, e.g., their Table 6). Nonetheless, Hanushek (in a personal communication) said he extracted only one estimate from this study because only one specification controlled explicitly for family background information, although all the estimates conditioned on race in the same fashion as Link and Mulligan's (1991) 24 estimates.[9]

Summers and Wolfe's (1977) *American Economic Review* article provides another example of a study that yielded only one estimate despite having reported multiple estimates for multiple samples. Summers and Wolfe analyzed data for 627 sixth-grade students in 103 elementary schools. They mention that data were also analyzed for 533 eighth-grade students and 716 12th-grade students, with similar class size results, but these results were not included in Hanushek's tabulation.[10] Summers and Wolfe (1986, Table 1) provide two sets of regression estimates: one with pupil-specific school inputs and another with school averages of school inputs. They also provide pupil-level estimates of class size effects estimated separately for subsamples of low-, middle-, and high-achieving students, based on students' initial test scores (see their Table 3). Hanushek selected only one estimate from this paper. Why the estimates reported for the various subsamples were excluded is unclear. In addition, because Hanushek (1991) draws inferences concerning the effect of the level of aggregation of the data on the estimates, it is unfortunate that results using both sets of input data (pupil level or school level) were not extracted. Contrary to Hanushek's conclusion about the effect of data aggregation, Summers and Wolfe (1977, 649) conclude, "when there are extensive pupil-specific data [on inputs] available, more impact from school inputs is revealed."

No estimates were selected from Finn and Achilles's (1990) published analysis of the STAR experiment. In a personal communication, Hanushek said that this decision was made because Finn and Achilles did not control for family background (other than race and school location). However, the STAR experiment used random assignment of students to classes, and econometric reasoning suggests that controls for family background should therefore be unnecessary (because family background variables and class size are expected to be uncorrelated).

Column 1 of **Table 1-2** summarizes Hanushek's tabulation of the estimates he selected from the literature. His approach equally weights all 277 estimates drawn from the underlying 59 studies. Following Hanushek, estimates that indicate that smaller classes are associated with better student performance are classified as positive results.[11] The bottom of the table reports the ratio of the number of positive to negative results. Below this is the p-value that corresponds to the probability of observing so high a ratio if, in fact, there were no relationship between class size and student performance and each study's results were merely a random draw with positive and negative results equally likely.[12] That is, how different are the results from a series of coin flips in which positive (heads) or negative (tails) results are equally likely in each study? A p-value of less than 0.05 indicates that the observed ratio of positive to negative results would occur by chance less than one time in 20, and is typically taken as evidence of a statistically significant relationship. Column 1, with a p-value of 0.500, indeed shows no systematic relationship between smaller classes and better student performance; estimates are virtually equally likely to be negative as positive. Only one quarter of the estimates are statistically significant, and these are also about equally likely to be negative as positive.

As mentioned, Hanushek's procedure places more weight on studies from which he extracted more estimates. There are a number of reasons to question the statistical properties of such an approach. First, studies that

TABLE 1-2   Reanalysis of Hanushek's (1997) literature summary of class size studies

Result	Hanushek weights (1)	Equally weighted studies (2)	Weighted by number of citations (3)	Selection-adjusted weighted studies (4)
Positive and stat. sig.	14.8%	25.5%	30.6%	33.5%
Positive and stat. insig.	26.7	27.1	21.1	27.3
Negative and stat. sig.	13.4	10.3	7.1	8.0
Negative and stat. insig.	25.3	23.1	26.1	21.5
Unknown sign and stat. insig.	19.9	14.0	15.1	9.6
Ratio positive to negative	1.07	1.57	1.56	2.06
P-value*	0.500	0.059	0.096	0.009

Note: See text for full explanation. Column (1) is from Hanushek (1997, Table 3), and implicitly weights studies by the number of estimates that were taken from each study. Columns (2), (3), and (4) are author's tabulations based on data from Hanushek (1997). Column (2) weights each estimate by one over the number of estimates taken from that study, thus weighting each study equally. Column (3) calculates a weighted average of the data in column (2), using the number of times each study was cited as weights. Column (4) uses the regressions in Table 1-3 to adjust for sample selection (see text). A positive result means that a smaller class size is associated with improved student performance. The table is based on 59 studies.

* P-value corresponds to the proportion of times the observed ratio, or a higher ratio, of positive to negative results would be obtained in 59 independent random draws in which positive and negative results were equally likely.

contain many estimates are likely to have broken their data into several subsamples, and as a result estimates based on subsamples are given extra weight. These estimates by definition have fewer observations — and higher sampling variances — than estimates based on the full samples, and an optimal weighting scheme should therefore give them *lower* weights.[13] Second, there is reason to suspect a systematic relationship between a study's findings and the number of estimates it contains. Most people expect there to be a positive relationship between small classes and test performance. Authors who find weak or negative results (e.g., because of sampling variability or specification errors) may be required by referees to provide additional estimates to probe their findings (or they may do so voluntarily), whereas authors who use a sample or specification that generates an expected positive effect may devote less effort to reporting additional estimates for subsamples. If this is the case, and if findings are not independent across estimates (as would be the case if a misspecified model is estimated on different subsamples), then Hanushek's weighting scheme will place too much weight on insignificant and negative results.

FIGURE 1A   Average percent of estimates positive, negative, or unknown sign, by number of estimates taken from study

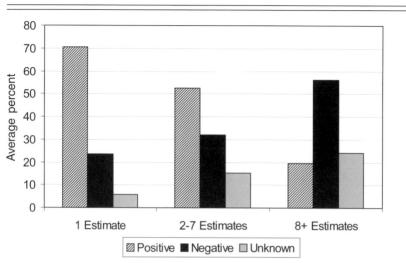

Notes: Based on data from Hanushek (1997). Arithmetic averages of percent positive, negative, and unknown sign are taken over the studies in each category.

A good argument could be made that Summers and Wolfe (1977) should have received more weight and Link and Mulligan (1986) less in Hanushek's literature summary. Weighting studies equally prevents any study with a large number of estimates from having a disproportionate influence on the overall representation of the literature.

Figure 1A provides evidence that Hanushek's procedure assigns excessive weight to studies with unsystematic or negative results. The figure shows the fraction of estimates that are positive, negative, or of unknown sign by the number of estimates Hanushek took from each study. For the vast majority of studies from which Hanushek took only a small number of estimates, there is a clear and consistent association between smaller class sizes and student achievement. In the 17 studies from which Hanushek took only one estimate, for example, more than 70% of the estimates indicate that students tend to perform better in smaller classes while only 23% indicate a negative effect. By contrast, in the nine studies from which Hanushek took eight or more estimates each — for a total of 123 estimates — the opposite pattern holds: small classes are more likely to be associated with lower performance.

Table 1-3 more formally explores the relationship between the number of estimates that Hanushek extracted from each study and their results.

TABLE 1-3   Regressions of percent of estimates positive or negative, and significant or insignificant, on the number of estimates used from each study

	Dependent variable:				
	Percent positive & significant (1)	Percent positive & insignificant (2)	Percent negative & significant (3)	Percent negative & insignificant (4)	Percent unknown sign & insignificant (5)
Intercept	35.7 (6.4)	27.4 (6.0)	7.4 (4.5)	21.0 (5.9)	8.5 (5.6)
Number of estimates used	-2.16 (0.96)	-0.07 (0.89)	0.62 (0.66)	0.44 (0.88)	1.18 (0.83)
R-square	0.08	0.00	0.01	0.00	0.03

Notes: Standard errors are shown in parentheses. Sample size is 59 studies. Dependent variable is the percent of estimates used by Hanushek in each result category. Unit of observation is a study.

Specifically, column 1 reports a bivariate regression in which the dependent variable is the percent of estimates in a study that are positive and statistically significant (based on Hanushek's classification), and the explanatory variable is the number of estimates that Hanushek took from the study. The unit of observation in the table is a study, and the regression is estimated for Hanushek's set of 59 studies. Columns 2-5 report analogous regressions where the dependent variable is the percent of estimates that are positive and insignificant, negative and significant, negative and insignificant, or of unknown sign, respectively. These results show that Hanushek's summary uses fewer estimates from studies that tended to find positive and significant results ($r = -0.28$), and this relationship is stronger than would be expected by chance alone. Moreover, the opposite pattern holds for studies with negative and significant findings: relatively more estimates from studies with perverse class size effects are included in the sample, although this relationship is not significant. Table 1-3, then, seems to provide strong evidence that Hanushek's selection criteria have the effect of biasing his representation of the literature toward finding zero or negative effect of class size on performance.

The rule that Hanushek used for selecting estimates would be expected to induce a positive association between the prevalence of insignificant results and the number of estimates taken from a study, since studies with more estimates probably used smaller subsamples (which are more likely to generate insignificant estimates). *But Table 1-3 also shows something different: that Hanushek took more estimates from studies that had nega-*

tive, statistically significant results. Sampling bias resulting from smaller subsamples cannot explain this, although one explanation may come from the refereeing process discussed above. In any case, given this aspect of Hanushek's estimate selection process, we should expect his results to be biased toward a negative or unsystematic effect of class size reduction; it is not surprising that he found little evidence for a positive effect.

The remaining columns of Table 1-2 attempt to remove the bias from Hanushek's procedure by weighting the different studies more appropriately. As a partial correction for the oversampling from studies with negative and insignificant estimates, in column 2 of Table 1-2 the underlying studies — as opposed to the individual estimates extracted from the studies — are given equal weight. This is accomplished by assigning to each study the percent of estimates that are positive and significant, positive and insignificant, and so on, and then taking the arithmetic average of these percentages over the 59 studies.[14] This simple and plausible change in the weighting scheme substantially alters the inference one draws from the literature. In particular, studies with positive effects of class size are 57% more prevalent than studies with negative effects.

In column 3 of Table 1-2 an alternative approach is used. Instead of weighting the studies equally, studies are weighted based on a measure of their quality, as indicated by the frequency with which they are cited. Studies are assigned a weight equal to the cumulative number of citations to the study as of August 1999, based on a "cited reference search" of the *Social Science Citation Index*. Column 3 presents the weighted mean of the percentages. Although there are obvious problems with using citations as an index of study quality (e.g., articles published earlier have more opportunity to be cited; norms and professional practices influence the number of citations, etc.), citation counts are a widely used indicator of quality, and should be a more reliable measure of study quality than the number of estimates Hanushek extracted. The results are similar to those in column 2: studies with statistically significant, positive findings outweigh those with statistically significant, negative findings by over 2 to 1.

Another alternative, and in some respects superior, approach to adjust for estimate selection bias is to use the regressions in Table 1-3 to generate predicted percentages for all studies under the hypothetical situation in which one estimate was provided by each study. This is akin to creating a simulated dataset that looks like Hanushek's data might have looked if he took only one estimate from each study. This approach would be preferable to the equally-weighted-studies approach in column 2 if the primary estimate in each study tends to be systematically different from the secondary estimates. Such a pattern could arise, for example, if the first estimate that each study presents is for its full sample, and subsequent estimates carve the sample into smaller subsamples that naturally yield noisier estimates. A linear approximation to what the average study would find if one estimate were extracted from all studies is derived by adding together the intercept and slope in each of the regression models in Table 1-3. These results predict what the outcome would have been if each study had reported only one estimate.[15] Column 4 of Table 1-2 reports the distribution of results using this simulated dataset. This approach for adjusting for the selection of estimates from the studies indicates even stronger and more consistent positive effects of class size. After adjusting for selection, studies with positive results are twice as likely as studies with negative results; if in fact there were no positive relationship between performance and small classes, the probability of observing this many studies with positive results by chance would be less than one in a hundred. Among studies with statistically significant results, positive results outnumber negative results by 4 to 1.

In sum, all three of these alternatives to Hanushek's weighting scheme produce results that point in the opposite direction of his findings: all three find that smaller class sizes are positively related to performance, and that the pattern of results observed in the 59 studies is unlikely to have arisen by chance. It should be emphasized that the results reported in Table 1-2 are all based on Hanushek's coding of the underlying studies. Although Hanushek (1997) tried to "collect information from all studies meeting" his selection criteria, he notes that "[s]ome judgment is required in selecting from among the alternative specifications." The selection and classification of estimates in many of the studies is open to question, and could in part account for the curious relationship between the number of estimates taken from a study and the study's findings. The following examples illustrate some additional types of problems encountered in the way studies were coded, and the limitations of some of the underlying estimates:

- As mentioned previously, the Link and Mulligan (1986) study was classified as having 24 statistically insignificant estimates of unknown sign, although the authors mention that class size was insignificant in only 12 of the equations they estimated, use a subsample of a larger dataset also used in another paper, and do not report tests for the joint significance of class size and peer group achievement (which typically indicate that smaller classes have beneficial effects in classes of low-ability students). The median sample size in this paper was 237, compared with 3,300 in Link and Mulligan (1991), yet all estimates received equal weight.

- Jencks and Brown (1975) analyze the effect of high school characteristics on students' educational attainment, but their sample is necessarily restricted to individuals who were continuously enrolled in high school between ninth and 12th grade. Thus, any effect of class size on high school dropout behavior — a key determinant of educational attainment — is missed in this sample.

- Kiesling (1967) was classified as having three estimates of the effect of class size, but there is no mention of a class size variable in Kiesling's paper.

- Burkhead's (1967) study yielded 14 estimates, all of which were statistically insignificant (three quarters were negative). Four of these estimates are from a sample of just 22 high-school-level observations in Atlanta.[16] Moreover, the outcome variable in some of the models, post-high-school-education plans, was obtained by "a show of hands survey in the high schools." Despite these limitations, with 14 estimates this study receives over three times as much weight as the median study in Hanushek's summary.

- At least a dozen of the studies that Hanushek included in his sample estimated regression models that included expenditures per pupil and teachers per pupil as separate regressors in the same equation (e.g., Maynard and Crawford 1976). The interpretation of the teachers-per-pupil variable in these equations is particularly problematic because one would expect the two variables (expenditures per pupil and teachers per pupil) to vary together. One can identify the separate effect of teachers per pupil only if they do not vary together, which is most likely to happen when there are differences between schools in teacher salaries. That is, if School A has a lower pupil-teacher ratio than School B, but the schools have equal expenditures per pupil, the most likely way School A achieved a lower pupil-teacher ratio is by paying its teachers less — a difference that obviously could influence student achievement.[17] Using this source of variability in class size obviously changes the interpretation of the class-size result, and renders the finding irrelevant for most policy considerations.

Expenditures per student

Hanushek (1997) also examines the effect of expenditures per student, although he argues that "studies involving per-pupil expenditure tend to be the lowest quality studies." **Table 1-4** is analogous to Table 1-2 for the

TABLE 1-4   Reanalysis of Hanushek's (1997) literature summary; studies of expenditures per pupil

Result	Hanushek weights (1)	Equally weighted studies (2)	Weighted by number of citations (3)	Selection-adjusted weighted studies (4)
Positive and stat. sig.	27.0%	38.0%	33.5%	50.5%
Positive and stat. insig.	34.3	32.2	30.5	29.7
Negative and stat. sig.	6.7	6.4	2.7	6.0
Negative and stat. insig.	19.0	12.7	14.8	5.5
Unknown sign and stat. insig.	12.9	10.7	18.4	8.3
Ratio positive to negative	2.39	3.68	3.66	6.97
P-value*	0.0138	0.0002	0.0002	0.0000

Notes: Column (1) is from Hanushek (1997, Table 3), and implicitly weights studies by the number estimates that were taken from each study. Columns (2), (3), and (4) are author's tabulations based on data from Hanushek (1997). Column (2) assigns each study the fraction of estimates corresponding to the result based on Hanushek's coding, and calculates the arithmetic average. Column (3) calculates a weighted average of the data in column (2), using the number of times each study was cited as weights. Column (4) uses regressions corresponding to Table 1-3 to adjust for sample selection (see text). A positive result means that a smaller class size is associated with improved student performance. The table is based on 41 studies.

* P-value corresponds to the proportion of times the observed ratio, or a higher ratio, of positive to negative results would be obtained in 41 independent Bernouli trials in which positive and negative results were equally likely.

expenditure-per-pupil studies. The first column uses Hanushek's method, which weights studies by the number of estimates he extracted from them. The second column equally weights each study. The third column weights the studies by the number of times the article has been cited, and the fourth column uses the regression-adjustment method described above. In all cases, the relative frequency of studies that find positive effects of expenditures per student is greater than would be expected by chance. A total of 163 estimates were extracted from 41 studies.

The following regression coefficients describe the relationship between the percent of estimates that are positive, negative, or of unknown sign, and the number of estimates represented by the study, for the 41 studies in Hanushek's summary. (Standard errors for the coefficients are in parentheses, and an asterisk indicates a statistically significant coefficient at the 0.10 level.)

Percent positive =   83.6* - 3.4* (number of estimates used) $R^2 = .09$
                     (8.9)   (1.7)

Percent negative = 8.9 + 2.6* (number of estimates used) $R^2 = .08$
                   (6.9) (1.3)

Percent unknown = 7.5 + 0.8 (number of estimates used) $R^2 = .01$
                  (7.6) (1.5)

As with the class size studies, Hanushek extracted more estimates from studies that tended to find insignificant or negative effects of expenditures per student and fewer from studies that found positive effects. The dependence between the number of estimates and a study's results accounts for why Hanushek's technique of weighting more heavily the studies from which he took more estimates produces the least favorable results for expenditures per student. All of the various weighting schemes in Table 1-4 indicate that greater expenditures are associated with greater student achievement.

Summing up

In response to work by Hedges, Laine, and Greenwald (1994), Hanushek (1996b, 69) argued that, "[u]nless one weights it in specific and peculiar ways, the evidence from the combined studies of resource usage provides the answer" that resources are unrelated to academic achievement, on average. Since Hanushek's results are produced by implicitly weighting the studies by the *number* of "separate" estimates they present (or more precisely, the number of estimates he extracted from the studies), it seems likely that the opposite conclusion is more accurate: unless one weights the studies of school resources in peculiar ways, the *average study* tends to find that more resources are associated with greater student achievement.

This conclusion does not, of course, mean that reducing class size is necessarily worth the additional investment, or that class size reductions benefit all students equally. These questions require knowledge of the strength of the relationships between class size and economic and social benefits, knowledge of how these relationships vary across groups of students, and information on the cost of class size reduction. These issues are taken up in the next section. But the results of this reanalysis of Hanushek's literature summary should give pause to those who argue that radical changes in public school incentives are required because school inputs are unrelated to school outputs. When the study is the unit of observation, Hanushek's coding of the literature suggests that class size is a determinant of student achievement, at least on average.

II. Economic criterion

Hanushek (1997, 144) argues that, "[g]iven the small confidence in just getting noticeable improvements [from school resources], it seems somewhat unimportant to investigate the size of any estimated effects." This argument is unpersuasive for at least two reasons. First, as argued above, Hanushek's classification of studies in the literature indeed provides evidence of a systematic relationship between school inputs and student performance for the typical school district. Second, if the estimates in the literature are imprecise (i.e., have large sampling variances), statistically insignificant estimates are not incompatible with large economic and social returns from reducing class size. The power of the estimates is critical: if a given study cannot statistically distinguish between a large positive effect of reducing class size and zero effect, it tells us little about the value of class size reductions. Statistical significance tells us only whether a zero effect can be rejected with confidence. But zero is not a very meaningful null hypothesis in this case: we would also be reluctant to spend large amounts of money to reduce class sizes if the effect on outcomes was positive but *small*. What would be a more meaningful null hypothesis? One way to approach this question is to estimate a break-even point — the minimum benefit to reducing class size that would justify its cost — and use this as a basis for comparison. This section provides calculations suggesting a reasonable null hypothesis for the effect of class size based on standard economic considerations, and compares this to the results of the STAR experiment.

Lazear's theory of class size

A recent paper by Edward Lazear (1999) lays out an insightful economic theory of class size. In essence, Lazear argues that students who attend a smaller class learn more because they experience fewer student disruptions during class time, on average. Such a result follows naturally if the probability of a child disrupting a class is independent across children. Lazear then quite plausibly assumes that disruptions require teachers to suspend teaching, creating a "negative externality" that reduces the amount of learning for everyone in the class. There may be other benefits to smaller classes as well. For example, it is possible that students who spend time in small classes learn to behave better with closer supervision, leading to a reduced propensity to disrupt subsequent classes. Lazear's model probably captures an important feature of class size, and yields a specific functional form for the education production function.

Another implication of Lazear's model is that the "optimal" class size is larger for groups of students who are well behaved, because these students are less likely to disrupt the class and therefore benefit less from a class size reduction than more disruptive students. Schools therefore have an incentive to assign weaker, more disruptive students to smaller classes. Compensatory education programs that provide more resources to lower-achieving schools could also be viewed as targeting resources to weaker students. If schools voluntarily assign weaker students to smaller classes (as predicted by Lazear) or if compensatory funding schemes cause weaker students to have smaller classes, a spurious negative association between smaller classes and student achievement would be created. This phenomenon could explain why studies that avoid this problem by focusing on changes in class size that are not chosen by school administrators but are imposed from outside for reasons unrelated to individual students — such as in Angrist and Lavy's (1999) clever analysis of Israel's Maimonides law, as well as the STAR experiment — tend to find that smaller classes have a beneficial effect on student achievement. For educational policy, the relevant parameter is the potential gain in achievement from exogenous reductions in class size from current levels, not the relationship estimated from observed variations in class sizes voluntarily chosen by schools.

One final aspect of Lazear's model is worth emphasizing. If schools behave optimally, then they will reduce class size to the point that the benefit of further reductions in class size just equals the cost.[18] This implication provides a plausible economic null hypothesis. If we are starting from the optimal level, the costs and benefits of changes in class size should be roughly equivalent. As Lazear (1999) writes, "The point is that even if class size effects are potentially important, in equilibrium, marginal changes in class size may have small effects on observed educational output. If large gains were available from lowering class size, then those changes would have been made." Unless large opportunities for social gain are left unexploited by local school districts, we would expect the benefits of further reductions in class size to equal their costs.

Benefits and costs of educational resources

Improved school resources can have many benefits for students. This section focuses on one particular potential benefit: the effect on students' future labor market earnings. Improved school resources might help students learn more and, separately, raise their educational aspirations. These can both pay off in the labor market, leading to better job placements and higher earnings within each job. This section attempts to quantify the size of this benefit by combining the effect of school resources on standardized test scores with the relationship between test scores and labor market earnings.

Several studies have examined the relationship between students' test scores while in school and their subsequent earnings. Three recent studies illustrate the magnitude of this relationship:

- Murnane, Willet, and Levy (1995), using data from the High School and Beyond survey, estimate that male high school seniors who scored one standard deviation (SD) higher on the basic math achievement test in 1980 earned 7.7% higher earnings six years later, and females earned 10.9% more. This study, however, also controls for students' eventual educational attainment, so any effect of test scores on educational attainment — which, of course, affects wages — is not attributed to the influence of test scores.

- Currie and Thomas (1999) use the British National Child Development Study to examine the relationship between math and reading test scores at age 7 and earnings at age 33. They find that students who score in the upper quartile of the reading exam earn 20% more than students who score in the lower quartile of the exam, while students in the top quartile of the math exam earn another 19% more.[19] Assuming that scores are normally distributed, the average student in the top quartile scores about 2.5 standard deviations higher than the average student in the bottom quartile, so these results imply that a one standard-deviation increase in reading test performance is associated with 8.0% higher earnings, while a one standard-deviation increase in the math test is associated with 7.6% higher earnings.

- Neal and Johnson (1996) use the National Longitudinal Survey of Youth to estimate the effect of students' scores on the Armed Forces Qualification Test (AFQT), taken at age 15-18, on their earnings at age 26-29. Adjusting for the students' age when the test was taken, they find that a one standard-deviation increase in scores is associated with about 20% higher earnings for both men and women.

There are probably three important reasons why Neal and Johnson find a larger effect of test scores on wages than do Currie and Thomas. First, Currie and Thomas use a test administered at age 7, while Neal and Johnson use a test administered when their sample was in its late teens. Currie and Thomas find some mean regression in test scores — students who score very high at young ages tend to have smaller score increases as they age than do students who score very low on the earlier test — which suggests that a later test might be a stronger predictor of earnings. Second, Neal and Johnson use only a single test score while Currie and Thomas use both reading and math scores, which are correlated. Finally, differences between British and American labor markets might account for part of the difference. Based on these three studies, a plausible assumption is that a one standard-deviation increase in either math or reading scores is associated with about 8% higher earnings.

From an investment perspective, the timing of costs and benefits is critical. The costs of hiring additional teachers and obtaining additional classrooms are borne up front, while the benefits are not realized until years later, after students join the labor market. Delayed benefits need to be discounted to make them comparable to up-front costs. To illustrate the benefits and costs, consider extending the STAR class size reduction experiment to the average U.S. student entering kindergarten in 1998. In the STAR experiment, classes were reduced from about 22 to about 15 students, so assume that funds are allocated to create 47% (7/15) more classes.

Probably a reasonable approximation is that the cost of creating and staffing more classrooms is proportional to the annual per pupil cost.[20] We assume for this cost-benefit calculation that the additional cost per pupil each year a pupil is in a small class equals $3,501, or 47% of $7,502, which was the nationwide total expenditures per student in 1997-98.[21] Although the STAR experiment lasted four years, the average student who was assigned to a small class spent 2.3 years in a small class.[22] We also assume the additional costs are $3,501 in years 1 and 2, 30% of $3,501 in year 3, and zero in year 4. Denoting the cost of reducing class size in year t as C_t, the present value (PV) of the costs discounted to the initial year (1998) using a real discount rate of r is:

$$PV \ of \ Costs = \sum_{t=1}^{4} C_t / (1+r)^t.$$

Column 2 of **Table 1-5** provides the present value of the costs for various values of the discount rate.

The economic benefits of reduced class size are harder to quantify, and occur further in the future. Suppose initially that the earnings of the current labor force represent the exact age-earnings profile that the average student who entered kindergarten in 1998 will experience when he or she completes school and enters the labor market. **Figure 1B** illustrates this age-earnings profile for workers in 1998.[23] The figure displays average annual earnings for workers at each age between 18 and 65. As is commonly found, earnings rise with age until workers reach the late 40s, peak in the early 50s, and then decline. Average earnings are quite low until workers reach their mid-20s. Let E_t represent the average real earnings each year after age 18.

TABLE 1-5　Discounted present value of benefits and costs of reducing class size from 22 to 15 in grades K-3 (1998 dollars)

Discount rate (1)	Cost (2)	Increase in income assuming productivity growth rate of:		
		None (3)	1% (4)	2% (5)
0.02	$7,787	$21,725	$31,478	$46,294
0.03	7,660	15,174	21,667	31,403
0.04	7,537	10,784	15,180	21,686
0.05	7,417	7,791	10,819	15,238
.06	7,300	5,718	7,836	10,889

NOTE: Figures assume that a one standard deviation increase in math test scores or reading test scores in grades K-3 is associated with an 8% increase in earnings, and that attending a small class in grades K-3 raises math and reading test scores by 0.20 SD. Real wages are assumed to grow at the same rate as productivity. Costs are based on the assumption that students are in a smaller class for 2.3 years, as was the average in the STAR experiment.

Assume that β represents the increase in earnings associated with a one standard-deviation increase in either math or reading test scores. The preceding discussion suggests that 8% is a reasonable estimate for the value of β. Now let δ_M and δ_R represent the increase in math and reading test scores (in standard-deviation units) due to attending smaller classes in grades K-3. The STAR experiment suggests that δ_M and $\delta_R = 0.20$ standard deviations is a reasonable figure to use (see, e.g., Finn and Achilles 1990 or Krueger 1999b). Then the average real earnings of students from smaller classes is $E_t \times (1 + \beta(\delta_M + \delta_R))$. This exceeds average real earnings of students from regular-size classes by $E_t \times \beta(\delta_M + \delta_R)$. The addition to annual earnings must be discounted back to the initial year to account for the fact that a dollar received in the future is less valuable than a dollar received today. Assuming students begin work at age 18 and retire at age 65, the appropriate formula for discounting the higher earnings stream due to smaller classes back to the beginning of kindergarten is:

$$PV \ of \ Benefits = \sum_{t=14}^{61} E_t \, x\beta(\delta_M + \delta_R) / (1 + r)^t.$$

Using these assumptions, column 3 of Table 1-5 reports the present value of the additional earnings due to reducing class size by seven students for various values of the discount rate.

One important issue, however, is that real average earnings are likely

FIGURE 1B   Age-earnings profile, 1998

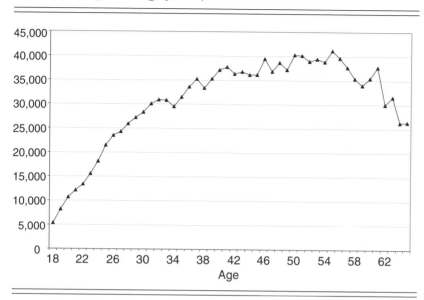

to grow substantially between 1998 and the year when the average kindergartner of 1998 retires. That is, when the kindergartners of 1998 enter the labor market, their average earnings (after adjusting for inflation) will be greater than that depicted in Figure 1B. Real wages typically grow in step with labor productivity (i.e., output per hour). Over the 20th century, real earnings and productivity have typically grown by 1% or 2% per year. The estimates of β discussed above are all based on earnings long after students started school, which reflect the effect of higher productivity growth on earnings. Consequently, columns 4 and 5 present discounted benefits assuming either 1% or 2% annual productivity and real wage growth after 1998.[24] The latest Social Security trustees' intermediate projection is for real wages to grow by slightly less than 1% per year over the next 75 years, so column 4 arguably probably provides a reasonable forecast of future earnings.

The next question is, which discount rate should one use to discount costs and benefits from age 5 until 65? The current yield on essentially risk-free long-term inflation-indexed government bonds is just under 4%. If we assume an interest rate of 4% (row 3), then the benefits of reducing class size from 22 to 15 in the early grades would be 43% greater than the costs absent real wage growth, and 100% greater than the costs if real wages grow by 1% per year. However, because the payoff to reduced class sizes is uncertain, society might desire to reflect some risk in the interest rate used to discount future benefits. A higher discount rate would then be desired. With a discount rate of 6% and 1% annual productivity growth, the costs of reducing class size from 22 to 17 students are predicted to almost equal the benefits, in line with Lazear's prediction.

An informed reader might question whether a 0.20 standard deviation gain from smaller classes is appropriate for the calculations in Table 1-5. In particular, work by Krueger and Whitmore (1999) and Nye, Zaharias, Fulton, et al. (1994) suggests that the improved test performance of small-class students in Project STAR may have fallen to about 0.10 standard deviations by the end of high school.[25] Although it is possible that some of the initial gain from small classes in the STAR experiment faded after students returned to regular-size classes, the calculations reported in Table 1-5 are probably still reasonable. The reason for this supposition is that Currie and Thomas's estimate of β is based on test scores at age 7. They find some regression to the mean in test scores as students age — that is, students with high scores at age 7 tend to drift lower, while students with low initial scores tend to see larger increases. This regression to the mean is consistent with the Krueger and Whitmore and Nye et al. results mentioned above. If the 0.10 SD gain in test scores at older ages is to be used in the calculations, then a higher value of β would be appropriate, as test scores of high school seniors are more strongly correlated with eventual earnings than are those students' scores at age 7.

The 'critical effect size'

Another, perhaps more relevant, way to consider the benefit-cost calculus is to ask, what is the minimum increase in test scores from a reduction in class size of seven students in grades K-3 that is required to justify the added cost? That is, at what size of the increase in test scores do the benefits of class size reduction exactly equal the costs? This "critical effect size" provides a logical null hypothesis for policy makers and researchers to use in evaluating the economic significance of the class size literature. The critical effect size was calculated by solving for δ^* in the following equation:

$$\sum_{t=1}^{4} C_t / (1+r)^t = \sum_{t=14}^{61} E_t \, x (.08)(2\delta^*) / (1+r)^t,$$

where math and reading scores are assumed to increase by the same amount due to smaller classes, and β has been fixed at 0.08.

Estimates of the "critical effect size" for various values of the discount rate and productivity growth are reported in **Table 1-6**. A noteworthy

TABLE 1-6 Required standard deviation increase in elementary school math and reading test scores for a class size reduction of seven students to break even

Discount rate (1)	Critical effect size assuming annual productivity growth rate:		
	None (2)	1% (3)	2% (4)
0.02	0.072	0.049	0.034
0.03	0.101	0.071	0.049
0.04	0.140	0.099	0.070
0.05	0.190	0.137	0.097
0.06	0.255	0.186	0.134

Note: Figures assume that a one standard deviation increase in math test scores or reading test scores in grades K-3 is associated with an 8% increase in earnings. Real wages are assumed to grow at the same rate as productivity.

finding is that the critical effect size is fairly small. If we use a 4% discount rate and expect 1% annual productivity growth, the minimum increase in elementary school math and reading scores required for the benefits to equal the costs of a class size reduction from 22 to 15 students is 0.10 standard deviations. The critical effect size for a class size reduction of one student, from 22 to 21, would be 0.010 standard deviations.[26] It seems likely that most of the estimates in the literature would have difficulty rejecting a critical effect size of this magnitude. Unfortunately, most studies do not provide sufficient information to test their results against this hypothesis.

Also notice that the effect sizes found in the STAR experiment and much of the literature are greater for minority and economically disadvantaged students than for other students. Although the critical effect size differs across groups with different average earnings, economic considerations suggest that resources would be optimally allocated if they were targeted toward those who benefit the most from smaller classes.

Caveats

Many assumptions underlying the cost-benefit calculations in Tables 1-5 and 1-6 could turn out to be wrong. The assumptions that are probably most critical are:

- The effect of test score gains on earnings in the future may turn out to be different than the value of β that was assumed. Indeed, because β was estimated from cross-section relations, it could reflect the effect of omitted characteristics, which would imply that it does not reflect the potential gain from increasing a particular student's scores.[27] In addition, general equilibrium effects could affect the value of β if class size is reduced on a wide scale — a substantial increase in the cognitive ability of the labor force would be expected to reduce the return to cognitive ability. It is also likely that school resources influence earnings by means that are not reflected in test scores. For example, class size may influence non-cognitive abilities, which are not reflected in test scores but nevertheless influence earnings, especially for blue-collar workers (see Cawley et al. 1996).

- Class size probably influences other outcomes with economic consequences, such as crime and welfare dependence, and there may be externalities from human capital, so the economic benefits could be understated. There are also non-economic benefits of improved education. None of these are captured by the focus here on individual earnings.

- It is unclear how much real earnings will grow in the future, although the 0-2% annual growth figures probably provide a reasonable range.

- The cost of reducing class size in the early grades may be different than assumed here. For example, expenditures per student are typically lower in grammar school, yet the analysis here uses expenditures per student in all grades as the basis for calculations. More importantly, the STAR experiment only reduced the number of classroom teachers, whereas the calculations here assume an across-the-board reduction in the number of teachers (including, e.g., physical education teachers, music teachers, and art teachers). Furthermore, the existence of fixed costs (e.g., administration, transportation) would also cause the assumption that costs are proportional to the number of teachers per pupil to overstate costs. These considerations suggest that the costs of class size reduction assumed here may have been substantially overstated.

- If class size is to be reduced on a wide scale, a great many new teachers will be needed to teach the new classes. In the short run, this could cause the quality of teachers to decline. On the other hand, more qualified individuals may be attracted to the teaching profession if classes are smaller.

- The calculations on workers' earnings in Tables 1-5 and 1-6 neglect fringe benefits, which are about 20% of total compensation. If fringe benefits increase in proportion to earnings, the reported benefits are understated by about 20%. The calculations also assume that everyone works for pay, at least part year, which tends to overstate the economic benefit, probably by 20% or so.

The related literature that directly examines the effect of expenditures per student on students' subsequent income provides some independent support for the calculations underlying Tables 1-5 and 1-6. Card and Krueger (1996) review 11 such studies. Although these studies are less well controlled than the STAR experiment, the median estimate is that a 10% increase in expenditures per student is associated with 1.25% higher earnings, and the inter-quartile range — the difference between the 75th percentile study and the 25th percentile study — is from 0.85% to 1.95%.[28] It turns out that this is quite close to the estimate derived above using the STAR experiment: if we assume linearity and $\beta=0.08$, then the STAR experiment implies that a 10% reduction in class size leads to a 1.0% increase in earnings.[29] Thus, despite employing quite different estimation procedures, the literature that directly estimates the effect of class size on earnings yields results that are in the same ballpark as the corresponding figure derived from the STAR experiment.

III. Conclusion

The method Hanushek uses to summarize the literature is often described as a "vote counting" exercise. The results are shown to depend critically on whether the approach allows *one study, one vote*. When studies are accorded equal weight, the literature exhibits systematic evidence of a relationship between class size and achievement. As implemented by Hanushek, however, studies from which multiple estimates were extracted are given multiple votes. No statistical theory is presented to support this weighting scheme, and it can be misleading. There are good reasons to think that this scheme leads to over-weighting studies with less systematic and less significant estimates. For example, other things equal, studies that report a larger number of estimates for finer subsamples will tend to yield less significant estimates, but will be given extra weight by Hanushek's weighting scheme. Studies are a more natural unit of observation, as it is studies, not estimates, that are accepted for publication. The importance of a study as the unit of observation is acknowledged by Hanushek's requirement that studies be published in a book or journal to assure a minimal quality check. The individual estimates that make up a study do not pass this quality hurdle in isolation: the combined weight of evidence in a study is evaluated to decide whether to publish it.

In view of the large differences between Hanushek's results and the results of the reanalysis undertaken here and in other meta-analyses, one should be reluctant to conclude that school resources are irrelevant to student outcomes. The strongest available evidence suggests a connection. In considering evidence on school resources and student achievement, it seems wise to raise the question asked by the Supreme Court of New Jersey in *Abbott v. Burke:* "[I]f these factors are *not* related to the quality of education, why are the richer districts willing to spend so much for them?"

Economics provides a useful framework for valuing the tradeoffs involved in increasing or decreasing class size. The calculations described in Section II, subject to the many caveats listed there, suggest that the economic benefits of further reductions in class size in grades K-3 are greater than the costs if a 4% real interest rate is used to discount benefits and costs to present values, and are about equal to the costs if a 6% real interest rate is used. With 1% per annum productivity growth and a 4% real discount rate, the "critical effect size" for the benefit of a reduction from 22 to 15 students to equal the costs is estimated to equal 0.10 standard deviations. This would be a natural hypothesis against which to test findings to judge their economic significance. Without knowing whether estimates are able to rule out the "critical effect size," it is difficult to assess the economic implications of the class size literature as a whole. The overall effect size from the STAR experiment, however, exceeds this critical effect size. Further, economic considerations suggest that greater gains might be available if resources were targeted toward those groups — minority and disadvantaged students — who appear to benefit the most from smaller classes.

Endnotes

1.   See Krueger (1999a).

2.   This quote is from Hanushek (1997, 148).

3.   The word "studies" is in quotation marks because the unit of observation in Hanushek's work is not an entire study, but rather an individual estimate, of which several might be drawn from a single study. This point is discussed more fully below.

4.   The distinction between studies and separate estimates is often blurred in the press. For example, an article in *Education Week* (April 12, 2000) on a class-size reduction program in Wisconsin reported that Eric Hanushek "has examined more than 275 similar studies."

5.   It is not uncommon for some of the estimates to be based on as few as 20 degrees of freedom (i.e., there are only 20 more observations than parameters to be identified), so the sampling errors can be very large.

6.   The same data are used in the literature summaries in Hanushek (1996a, 1996b, and 1998).

7.   Many of these studies reported more than one estimate, but only one estimate was selected because the separate estimates may not have been deemed sufficiently different in terms of sample or specification. Hanushek (1997) notes that as a general rule he tried to "reflect the estimates that are emphasized by the authors of the underlying papers."

8.   It is unclear how Hanushek derived 24 estimates of unknown sign from this study, however, because no mention of the class size variable was made in connection to the equations for the reading scores.

9.   In the Card and Krueger study, controlling for the income and education of parents leads to a slight increase in the effect of class size reductions on the rate of return to schooling.

10.   Their paper mentions that a full set of estimates for the additional samples was included in a Philadelphia Federal Reserve Bank publication, but this paper was not included in Hanushek's sample. Their footnote 22 also provides some description of the class size results in the other samples.

11.   I also follow the practice of using the terms "class size" and "pupil-teacher ratio" interchangeably. The difference is primarily a question of how one aggregates microdata.

12.   The p-value was calculated assuming 59 independent Bernoulli trials, from the 59 studies used. If instead the number of independent Bernoulli trials was 277 — the number of estimates Hanushek extracted from the literature — the p-value in column 1 would be 0.32.

13.   If the weights were selected to minimize the sampling variance of the combined estimate, the optimal weights would be the inverse of the sampling variances of the individual estimates (see Hedges and Olkin 1985).

14.   For example, if a study was classified as having one estimate that was positive and significant and one that was positive and insignificant, these two categories would each be assigned a value of 50%, and the others would be assigned 0. If a study reported only

one estimate, the corresponding category would be assigned 100% for that study.

15.   The dependent variable in column 1, for example, is the percentage of a study's estimates that are positive and statistically significant; the independent variable is the number of estimates. Therefore, the intercept gives the expected percentage positive and significant if there are zero estimates. Adding the slope gives the expected percentage if exactly one estimate is extracted per study. Obviously, in a study with only one estimate, either zero or 100% of the estimates will be positive and significant. The expected percentage for one estimate per study can be interpreted as the probability that a study's single estimate will be positive and significant, or as the fraction of single-estimate studies that we expect to have positive and significant results. These expected percentages are reported in column 4 of Table 1-2.

16.   Models estimated with this sample included eight explanatory variables and an intercept, so there were only 13 degrees of freedom. This is quite low, and would typically lead to very imprecise estimates.

17.   This type of problem arises in many estimates that Hanushek uses because the underlying studies were not designed to study the effect of class size, *per se*, but some other feature of the education process. Maynard and Crawford, for example, were interested in the effect of exogenous shifts in family income (arising from income maintenance experiments) on children's academic outcomes, and the study provides persuasive results on this issue; class size and expenditures per pupil were just ancillary variables that the researchers held constant.

18.   The assumption of optimal behavior by schools is supported by the theory of Tiebout sorting, in which it is an expected result of competition among municipalities. If, on the margin, parents chose where to live based on the schools, then one would expect schools to behave optimally. This, of course, stands in direct contradiction to the claims of Chubb and Moe (1990) and Finn (1991), who argue that schools do not optimize because their administrators are unaccountable and free of competition.

19.   These results come from a multiple regression with the log of the wage as the dependent variable and indicators for the reading and math scores in the upper and lower quartiles as explanatory variables. Currie and Thomas also estimate separate regressions for men and women, controlling in these models for father's occupation, father's education, number of children and birth order, mother's age, and birth weight. The wage gap between those who score in the top and bottom quartiles on the reading exam in these models is 13% for men and 18% for women, and on the math exam it is 17% for men and 9% for women. This suggests that only a modest part of the observed relationship between test scores and earnings results from differences in student background.

20 Folger and Parker (1990) tentatively conclude from the STAR experiment that proportionality is a reasonable assumption.

21.   See *Digest of Education Statistics, 1998*, Table 169.

22.   Students spent less than four years in a small class because half the students entered the experiment after the first year, and because some students moved to a new school or repeated a grade, causing them to return to regular size classes.

23.   The figure is based on data from the March 1999 Current Population Survey. The sample consists of all civilian individuals with any work experience in 1998.

24.   Formally, the average real wage for a worker who reaches age A in year t, denoted Y, is calculated by $Y = E (1+g)t$, where E is the average earnings in Figure 1B for a worker of age A and g is the rate of productivity growth.

25.   This could be because students assigned to small classes lost ground as they progressed through the later grades, or because students initially assigned to regular classes caught up to the small-class students.

26.   Because the costs are proportional to the teacher-pupil ratio, not to the number of students per teacher, the critical effect size for a one-student reduction varies depending on the initial class size.

27.   Note, however, that Jencks and Phillips (1999) find that math test score gains between 10th and 12th grade have about the same impact on subsequent earnings as cross-sectional differences in scores of equivalent magnitude in 10th grade.

28.   Betts (1996) similarly finds that the mean estimate in this literature is 1.04% higher earnings for 10% greater spending.

29.   This was calculated by $0.010 = 0.08*0.20*2*0.1/(7/22)$. One difficulty in comparing these two literatures, however, is that it is unclear how long class size is reduced in the observational studies on earnings. In some studies, the pupil-teacher ratio during a student's entire elementary and secondary school career is used, while in others just one year's data are used.

CHAPTER 2

Evidence, politics, and the class size debate

Eric A. Hanushek

With the suddenness of a summer storm, politics thrust the issue of class size policy onto the national agenda. Before the political popularity to voters of reductions in class size became known, most educational researchers and policy makers had discarded such policies as both too expensive and generally ineffective, leaving only teachers unions and others with clear vested interests in the policies to support such ideas. When the political appeal of class size reductions became known — largely through the reactions to the 1996 California policies — there was a scramble to backfill evidence supporting such policies. In this current environment, the evidence about the effectiveness of class size reduction has been thoroughly spun in the political debate in order to match the preconceived policy proposals, making it difficult to conclude that the debate has been guided very much by the evidence.

This political backdrop is necessary to understand the significance of Alan Krueger's reanalysis (in chapter 1) of the existing evidence on class size. He focuses attention directly on the scientific evidence and its implications for policy, thus attempting to move the policy debate away from pure politics and toward a better basis for decision making. While he offers no new evidence on the effects of class size on student performance, he contributes two different analyses that point toward a more aggressive policy of class size reduction: a massaging of the econometric evidence on effectiveness of class size reduction and of overall spending and a proposed demonstration that small outcome effects are still worthwhile. Upon careful inspection, however, neither is convincing. Nonetheless, policy makers should not ignore the emphasis on the importance of a solid evidentiary base.

Because supporters of class size reductions are likely to be attracted to his defense of such policies, it is important to understand the nature and substance of his analysis. First, his discussion omits mention of the long history and dismal results of class size policies. Second, his analysis of the existing econometric evidence derives its results from giving excessive weight to low-quality and biased estimates. Moreover, the analysis totally disregards the statistical significance of the various econometric estimates in attempting to make the case for support of overall class size reduction policies. Third, the discussion of the Tennessee STAR (Student/Teacher Achievement Ratio) experiment does not make clear its limited evidence for any broad reductions and fails to indicate the uncertainty surrounding the results and their policy implications. Finally, the calculation of benefit-cost relationships takes a very narrow view of potential policies and requires a number of heroic assumptions. This set of comments discusses each of these in turn.

The issue of course is not whether there exists any evidence that class size reduction *ever* matters. Surely class size reductions are beneficial in specific circumstances — for specific groups of students, subject matters, and teachers. The policy debates, driven by the politics of the situation, do not, however, attempt to identify any such specific situations but instead advocate broad reductions in class sizes across all schools, subjects, and often grades. The missing elements are three. First, nothing in the current decision process encourages targeting class size reductions to situations where they are effective. Second, class size reductions necessarily involve hiring more teachers, and teacher quality is much more important than class size in affecting student outcomes. Third, class size reduction is very expensive, and little or no consideration is given to alternative and more productive uses of those resources.

Similarly, while some have characterized my past research as indicating that "money makes no difference," this summary is inaccurate and misleading. My research and that of others shows that there are large differences among teachers and schools — differences that should be in my opinion the focus of aggressive public policy. At the same time, the organization of schools and the attendant incentives to improve student performance have been shown to distort the gains that could potentially come from added resources to schools. While some schools may use added resources to improve student outcomes, others will not. Moreover, we do not have the ability to predict which schools and which uses of additional funds will be effective. Therefore, the correct summary is "just providing more

TABLE 2-1   Pupil-teacher ratio and real spending, 1960-95

	1960	1970	1980	1990	1995
Pupil-teacher ratio	25.8	22.3	18.7	17.2	17.3
Current expenditure per pupil (1996/97 $)	$2,122	$3,645	$4,589	$6,239	$6,434

resources — whether in the form of reduced class sizes or in other forms — is unlikely to lead to higher student achievement as long as future actions of schools are consistent with their past choices and behavior."

The appeal of class size reduction is that it offers the hope of improving schools while requiring no change in the existing structure. Politicians can take credit for pursuing identifiable policies aimed at improving student outcomes. Teachers and other school personnel see added resources coming into schools without pressures to take responsibility for student performance and see these policies increasing the demand for teachers. The missing element is any reasonable expectation that these policies will significantly improve student achievement.

I. The history of class size reduction

Perhaps the most astounding part of the current debates on class size reduction is the almost complete disregard for the history of such policies. Pupil-teacher ratios fell dramatically throughout the 20th century.[1] **Table 2-1** shows that pupil-teacher ratios fell by a third between 1960 and 1995 — exceeding the magnitude of policy changes that most people are talking about today. With such substantial changes, one would expect to see their effect in student performance. Yet it is impossible to detect any overall beneficial effects that are related to these sustained increases in teacher intensity.

The longest general data series on student performance, albeit imperfect, is the Scholastic Aptitude Test (SAT). **Figure 2-A** displays the relationship between pupil-teacher ratios and SAT scores. While there is a relationship between the two, it goes in the opposite direction expected: reductions in pupil-teacher ratios are accompanied by falls in the SAT, even when appropriately lagged for the history of schooling experience for each cohort of students. Because the SAT is a voluntary test taken by a select population, a portion of the fall undoubtedly reflects changes in the test-taking population instead of real declines in aggregate student performance, but there is general consensus that real declines also occurred (Congressional Budget Office 1986).

FIGURE 2A   Pupil-teacher ratios and student performance

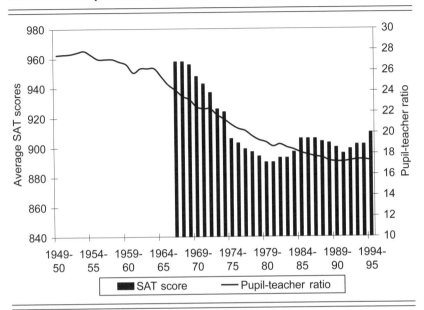

A better indicator of performance is the National Assessment of Educational Progress (NAEP). While tracking a representative sample of students, scores are available only since the early 1970s (after a period of substantial decline as measured by the SAT). **Figure 2-B** plots NAEP scores for 17-year-olds.[2] Math and reading show almost flat performance from earliest testing through 1999, while the comparable science and writing scores have declined significantly.[3] Thus, the consistent picture from available evidence is that the falling pupil-teacher ratios (and commensurately increasing real spending per pupil) have not had a discernible effect on student achievement.

While it is generally difficult to infer causation from aggregate trends, these data provide a strong *prima facie* case that the policies being discussed today will not have the significant outcomes that are advertised. The complication with interpreting these trend data is that other factors might work to offset an underlying beneficial effect. On this, the available evidence does not indicate that the pattern of test scores simply reflects changing student characteristics. Child poverty and the incidence of children in single-parent families — factors that would be expected to depress achievement — have risen. At the same time, the increases in parental education and the fall in family sizes would be expected to produce improvements in student performance. Netting out these effects is difficult to do with any

FIGURE 2B   National assessment of educational progress, 17 year-olds

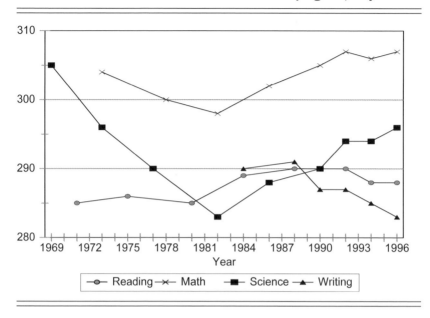

precision, but the existing analysis suggests little aggregate effect from the changing student backgrounds, and possibly a small net improvement.[4]

Table 2-1 also shows the significant increases in expenditure per pupil that have occurred over this period. A significant part of the increase in expenditure can be directly attributable to declines in the pupil-teacher ratio (Hanushek and Rivkin 1997), but other "improvements" such as having a more experienced and educated teacher force also contribute. Again, however, a comparison of student performance with the increases in inflation-adjusted expenditures of over 75% between 1970 and 1995 gives no reason to believe that more of the past resource policies will be successful.

If past declines in class size have had no discernible effect on student outcomes, why should we believe that future declines would yield any different results?

II. Econometric evidence

In his essay in this volume, Krueger concentrates most of his attention on the existing econometric evidence. While worrying about important issues, the analysis actually involves a set of calculations that places the heaviest weight on lower-quality estimates. By doing so, he is able to suggest that the overall conclusions about class size policies should change. If, how-

TABLE 2-2   Percentage distribution of estimated effect of teacher-pupil ratio and spending on student performance

		Statistically significant		Statistically Insignificant		
Resource	Number of estimates	Positive	Negative	Positive	Negative	Unknown sign
Teacher-pupil ratio	277	14%	14%	27%	25%	20%
Expenditure per pupil	163	27	7	34	19	13

Source: Hanushek (1997), as corrected (see appendix).

ever, more weight is placed on higher-quality estimates, the overall conclusion about a lack of clear relationship between class size and student performance is strengthened.

The misleading Krueger presentation

The starting point of Krueger's work is my prior tabulations of the estimated relationship between teacher-pupil ratios on student performance, as reproduced in **Table 2-2**.[5] The 277 separate estimates of the class size relationship are found in 59 publications, representing all of the available analyses through 1994. (Issues about the underlying data raised by Krueger in chapter 1 do not change any of the results, and a discussion of them is included in the appendix to these comments).

Among the statistically significant estimates — the ones for which we are reasonably confident that there is truly a relationship — 14% indicate that raising the teacher-pupil ratio would have the "expected" positive relationship, while an equal percentage indicate just the opposite. The statistically insignificant estimates — those for which we have less confidence that they indicate any real relationship — are almost evenly split between beneficial and adverse effects. (Note: one-fifth of the estimates, labeled "statistically insignificant – unknown sign," were not even described in terms of the direction of effect, even though they clearly add information about the lack of confidence in a consistent effect of class size). Thus, the overall evidence provides little reason to believe that a general policy of class size reduction would improve student performance.

Krueger questions these conclusions by arguing that individual publications that include more separate estimates of the impact of class size on performance are lower in quality than those publications that include fewer estimates.[6] His hypothesis is that publications including more estimates will involve splitting the underlying samples of student outcomes, say by race

TABLE 2-3   Sample sizes for estimated effect of teacher-pupil ratio by number of estimates per publication

Number of estimates per publication	Number of estimates (publications)	Sample size			
		Median	Average	Minimum	Maximum
1	17 (17)	272	1,310	48	14,882
2-3	28 (13)	649	1,094	47	5,000
4-7	109 (20)	512	2,651	38	18,684
8-24	123 (9)	266	1,308	22	10,871
1-24	277 (59)	385	1,815	22	18,684

or grade level. Statistical theory indicates that, other things being equal, smaller samples will yield less precise estimates than larger samples. He then jumps to the logically incorrect conclusion that publications with more individual estimates will tend to have fewer observations and thus will tend to produce statistically insignificant results when compared to those publications with fewer separate estimates.

There is no clear relationship between the sample sizes underlying individual estimates and the number of estimates in each publication. **Table 2-3** shows the distribution of sample sizes for the 277 estimates of the effect of teacher-pupil ratios from Table 2-2. While highly variable, publications with the fewest estimates do not systematically have the largest sample sizes. The simple correlation of sample sizes and number of articles in the underlying publications is slightly positive (0.03), although insignificantly different from zero.[7]

Before considering the precise nature of Krueger's re-analysis, it is useful to understand better the structure of the underlying estimates and publications. The explanation for varying numbers of estimates across individual publications is best made in terms of the provision of logically distinct aspects of the achievement process. For example, few people argue that the effects of class size reduction are constant across all students, grades, and subject matter. Therefore, when the data permit, researchers will typically estimate separate relationships for different students, different outcomes, and different grades. In fact, the analysis of the Tennessee class size experiment in Krueger (1999) divides the estimates by race and economic status, because Krueger himself thought it was plausible that class size has varying impacts — something that he finds and that he argues is important for policy. He further demonstrates varying effects by grade level. If there are different effects for different subsamples of students, then providing a single estimate across the subsamples, as advocated by Krueger and described below, is incorrect from a statistical point of view and would lead to biased results. Even though it is always possible to average across diverse effects, it would generally not be possible to use the estimates to understand the implications of class size reduction policies for different populations of students.

Even if class size differences have similar effects across students, districts, and outcomes, it is often impossible to combine the separate samples used for obtaining the individual estimates. For example, the publication by Burkhead et al. (1967) that Krueger holds up as an example of multiple estimates for small samples presents a series of estimates for high school performance in different cities where outcomes are measured by entirely different instruments. There is no way in which these can be aggregated into a single estimate of the effect of class size. Of the 59 publications from Table 2-2 that include estimates of the effects of the teacher-pupil ratio, 34 include two or more separate test measures of outcomes (e.g., reading and math), and 15 of these further include two or more separate non-test measures (e.g., college continuation, dropouts, or the like). For 14 of the 59 publications, the separate estimates of pupil-teacher effects within individual publications include students separated by more than three grade levels, implying not only different achievement tests but also the possibility of varying effects across grades. No general procedure exists for aggregating these separate effects in a single econometric estimate.

Thus, while Krueger suggests that the publication of multiple estimates is largely whimsical and misguided, the reality is that there are generally sound econometric reasons behind many of these decisions. The typical publication with several estimates actually provides more evidence than would be the case if only one estimate per publication were reported.

Krueger's hypothesis, however, is that an estimate in publications with more than one estimate provides poorer information than an estimate from a single-estimate publication. His analytical approach involves adding up the underlying estimates in alternative ways — effectively giving increased weight to some estimates and decreased weight to others. Specifically, he calculates the proportion of estimates within each publication that fits into the outcome categories (columns) in Table 2-2 and adds them up across the 59 separate publications, i.e., weighting by individual publications instead of individual estimates of the effect of class size on student performance. Surprisingly, this procedure leads to stronger support for the existence of positive effects from class size reduction, even though the simple statistical theory outlined by Krueger suggests that only the confidence in the estimates and not the direction of the relationship should be affected. The evidence based on the estimates in Table 2-2 indicates an essentially identical

FIGURE 2C   Estimates for teacher-pupil ratio with alternative weighting

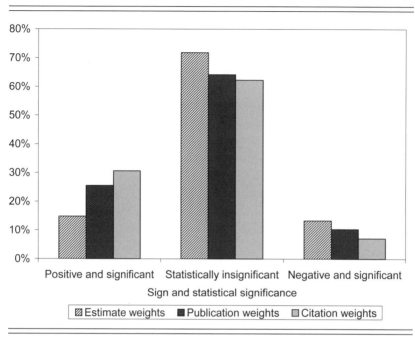

chance of finding increased teacher-pupil ratios to be beneficial as a chance of being harmful; i.e., no systematic relationship between class size and student outcomes. When re-weighted, however, Krueger finds beneficial effects to be noticeably more likely.

Note, however, that still only 25% of the time would there be much confidence that there is a relationship between teacher-pupil ratios and achievement as indicated by their being a statistically significant and positive estimate. To reach his conclusions of different overall results, Krueger tends to emphasize the proportion of estimates that are positive (beneficial) versus negative (detrimental), while completely ignoring the 20% of the estimates that are statistically insignificant but with an unknown sign.[8] This summary has a major problem. The equal weighting of statistically significant estimates (those more precisely estimated) and statistically insignificant estimates (less precisely estimated) seems to violate the basic premise of his re-weighting. A more accurate picture of the impact of his weighting is seen in **Figure 2-C**, which graphs the proportion of results that are statistically significant (positive or negative) and that are statistically insignificant.[9] His re-weighting produces a somewhat higher proportion of positive and statistically significant results, but it does not reverse the overall picture of little reason to expect much if any impact from reducing class size.

To deal with the apparent anomaly of finding different results (by sign of the estimates) when re-weighted, Krueger introduces a "theory of refereeing" for scholarly publications. He suggests that, whenever an author finds results that are statistically insignificant or that have the wrong sign, referees will insist that the author re-do the estimates by disaggregating them — in effect producing more of the insignificant or wrong-signed estimates.

While Krueger provides no evidence for his theory of refereeing, many — including Krueger himself — have argued just the opposite about the publication process. Specifically, there is a well-known publication bias toward having too many statistically significant estimates in articles that get published. Articles with insignificant estimates or incorrect signs simply do not get published with the same frequency as articles containing significant estimates of the expected sign (Hedges 1990). Krueger's own argument in discussing the literature on the minimum wages is "reviewers and editors have a natural proclivity to look favorably on studies that report statistically significant results" (Card and Krueger 1995, 186).

The importance of quality
Krueger is correct about the importance of quality of the estimates in formulating overall conclusions, and consideration of quality provides a much more natural and persuasive explanation for his altered results than does his theory of refereeing. The basic tabulation of results produced in Table 2-2 provided information on all available estimates of the effects of class size and of spending. The complete data are displayed not as an endorsement of uniform high quality but as a base case where there can be no possibility that selection of specific estimates and publications drives the results. At the same time, the underlying analyses clearly differ in quality, and — as discussed in Hanushek (1997) — these differences have the potential for biasing the results of the estimation.

Two elements of quality are particularly important. First, education policy in the United States is made primarily by the separate 50 states, and the variations in spending, regulations, graduation requirements, testing, labor laws, and teacher certification and hiring policies are large. These important differences — which are also the locus of most current policy debates — imply that any analyses of student performance across states must include descriptions of the policy environment of schools or else they will be subject to standard statistical bias problems, i.e., they will tend to obtain estimates that are systematically different from reality. Second, education is a cumulative process going across time and grades, but a majority of estimates consider only the current resources available to students in a given grade. For example, when looking at performance at the end of secondary schooling, many analyses rely on just the current teachers and school resources and ignore the dozen or more prior years of inputs. Obviously, current school inputs will tend to be a very imperfect measure of the resources that went into producing ending achievement.

While judgments about quality of an analysis generally have a subjective element, it is possible to make an initial cut based on the occurrence of these two problems. We begin with the issue of not measuring the state policy environment. If, as most people believe, states vary in important aspects of education policy and school operations, ignoring this in the econometric estimation will generally lead to biased estimates of the effect of teacher-pupil ratios or other resources. When important factors are omitted, estimates of the effect of varying teacher-pupil ratios will be unbiased *only if* there is no relationship across states between the quality of state policies and the average teacher-pupil ratio in the states. If on the other hand states with favorable education policies tend generally to have smaller classes, the estimates of teacher-pupil ratios will tend to differ systematically from the true effect of class size differences. The key is separating the true effects of teacher-pupil ratios from other attributes of schools and families, and this generally cannot be done accurately if the other factors are not explicitly considered. Whether the estimates tend to find too large or too small an effect of teacher-pupil ratios depends on the correlation of the omitted state regulatory and finance factors and class size (or spending).

The existing estimates contained in Table 2-2 can be used to identify the importance of biases caused by omitting consideration of differences in the state policy environment for schools. Specifically, an analysis that looks at schools entirely contained within a single state will observe a policy environment that is largely constant for all schools — and thus the econometric estimates that compare schooling entirely within a single state will not be biased. On the other hand, an analysis that considers schools in multiple states will produce biased results whenever important state differences in policy are correlated with differences across states in pupil-teacher ratios or overall resources. Moreover, the statistical bias will be largest for investigations relying on aggregate state data as opposed to observations at the classroom or school level.[10]

Thus, one clear measure of estimate quality is that it relies upon data entirely within a single state. For those using multistate data, estimates derived from the most aggregated data will be of lower quality than those relying on observed resources and outcomes at the classroom or school level.

TABLE 2-4   Percentage distribution of estimated effect of teacher-pupil ratio and expenditure per pupil by state sampling scheme and aggregation

Level of aggregation of resources	Number of estimates	Statistically significant		Statistically insignificant
		Positive	Negative	
A. Teacher-pupil ratio				
Total	277	14%	14%	72%
Single state samples[a]	157	11	18	71
Multiple state samples[b]	120	18	8	74
Disaggregated within states[c]	109	14	8	78
State-level aggregation[d]	11	64	0	36
B. Expenditure per pupil				
Total	163	27%	7%	66%
Single state samples[a]	89	20	11	69
Multiple state samples[b]	74	35	1	64
Disaggregated within states[c]	46	17	0	83
State-level aggregation[d]	28	64	4	32

a. Estimates from samples drawn within single states.
b. Estimates from samples drawn across multiple states.
c. Resource measures at level of classroom, school, district, or county, allowing for variation within each state.
d. Resource measures aggregated to state level with no variation within each state.

Table 2-4 provides a tabulation of the prior econometric results that is designed to illuminate the problem of ignoring the large differences in school organization and policy across states. The prior tabulation of all estimates shows that those with significant negative estimates evenly balance the percentage indicating teacher-pupil ratios with significant positive estimates. But Table 2-4 shows that this is not true for estimates relying upon samples drawn entirely within a single state, where the overall policy environment is constant and thus where any bias from omitting overall state policies is eliminated. For single-state analyses, the statistically significant effects are disproportionately negative (18% negative versus 11% positive). Yet, when the samples are drawn across states, the relative proportion that is positive and statistically significant rises. For those aggregated to the state level, almost two-thirds of the estimates are positive and statistically significant. The pattern of results also holds for estimates of the effects of expenditure differences (where positive and statistically significant estimates are most likely to come from investigations involving both multiple states and data aggregated to the state level).[11] Again, the vast majority of estimates are statistically insignificant or negative in sign except for those employing

TABLE 2-5 Percentage distribution of estimates of teacher-pupil ratio on student performance, based on value-added models of individual student performance

	Number of estimates	Statistically significant		Statistically insignificant
		Positive	Negative	
All	798	11%	9%	80%
Estimates for single state samples	24	4%	17%	79%

aggregated state-level data and neglecting differences in state policy environments. This pattern of results is consistent with expectations from considering specification biases when favorable state policies tend to be positively correlated with resource usage, i.e., when states with the best overall education policies also tend to have larger teacher-pupil ratios and higher spending.

The second problem is that the cumulative nature of the educational process means that relating the level of performance at any point in time just to the current resources is likely to be misleading. The mismeasurement is strongest for any children who changed schools over their careers. Each year some 20% of students switch schools. By the end of schooling a sizable majority of U.S. students have changed schools (for reasons other than normal moves across schooling levels). But mismeasurement also holds for students who do not move because of variations over time in school and family factors. While there is no general theoretical prediction about the biases that arise from such mismeasurement, its importance again can be understood by concentrating on estimates that do not suffer from the problem. The standard econometric approach for dealing with this is the estimation of value-added models where the statistical estimation is restricted to the growth of achievement over a limited period of time (where the flow of resources is also observed). By concentrating on achievement gains over, say, a single grade, it is possible to control for initial achievement differences (which will have been determined by earlier but generally unobserved resources and other educational inputs).

Table 2-5 displays the results of teacher-pupil ratio estimates that consider value-added models for individual students. The top panel shows all such results, while the bottom panel follows the earlier approach of concentrating just on estimates within an individual state. The top panel, which ignores problems of sampling across states, indicates slightly more estimates that are positive and statistically significant (11%) than those that are negative and statistically significant (9%), but the vast majority again provide little confidence that there is any systematic relationship (80%). With the most refined investigation of quality in the bottom panel, the number of estimates gets quite small and selective. In these, however, there is essentially no support for a conclusion that higher teacher-pupil ratios improve student performance. Only one of the available 24 estimates (4%) shows a positive and statistically significant relationship with student outcomes, while 17% find a negative and statistically significant relationship.

Finally, as noted previously, teacher-pupil ratios and class size are not the same measure, even though they tend to move together. The general estimation in Table 2-2 makes no distinction between the two measures. In the case of estimation at the individual classroom level (the focus of Table 2-5), however, the teacher-pupil ratio is essentially the same as class size. Thus, those measurement issues cannot distort these results. On the other hand, this distinction has its largest impact on differences across states, where state regulations, programs, and staffing policies imply variations in teacher-pupil ratios that are not necessarily matched by variations in typical class sizes. This measurement concern simply reinforces the previously mentioned problems with estimates derived from data gathered across different states.

The source of difference in tabulations of results

This direct analysis of quality of varying estimates shows why Krueger gets different effects from weighting results by publication instead of by individual estimates. From Table 2-2, 17 of the 59 publications (29%) contained a single estimate of the effect of the teacher-pupil ratio — but these estimates are only 6% of the 277 total available estimates. Krueger wants to increase the weight on these 17 estimates (publications) and commensurately decrease the weight on the remaining 260 estimates. Note, however, that over 40% of the single-estimate publications use state aggregate data, compared to only 4% of all estimates.[12] Relatedly, the single-estimate publications are more likely to employ multistate estimates (which consistently ignore any systematic differences in state policies) than the publications with two or more estimates. Weighting by publications rather than separate estimates, as Krueger promotes, heavily weights low-quality estimates.

The implications are easy to see within the context of the two publications that Krueger himself contributes (Card and Krueger 1992a, 1992b). Each of these state-level analyses contributes one positive, statistically significant estimate of the effect of teacher-pupil ratios. Weighting by all of the available estimates, these estimates represent 0.7% of the available estimates, but, weighting by publications, as Krueger desires, they represent 3.4%. Krueger (in chapter 1 of this volume) goes on to say that Card and Krueger (1992a) "presented scores of estimates for 1970 and 1980 Census samples sometimes exceeding one million observations. Nonetheless, Hanushek extracted only one estimate from this study because only one specification included family background information." This statement is quite misleading, however. While the underlying Census data on earnings included over a million observations, the relevant estimate of the effects of class size in Card and Krueger (1992a) relies on *just 147 state aggregate data points* representing different time periods of schooling. None of the estimates based on larger sample sizes is relevant for this analysis because each with a large sample fails to meet the eligibility criteria related to separating family background effects from correlated school resources (see below). In simple statistical terms, large samples cannot make up for estimating incorrectly specified relationships.

Krueger's statement also implies that requiring information on family backgrounds is some sort of irrelevant technicality. There are, however, very important econometric reasons for insisting on the inclusion of family background as a minimal quality requirement. It is well known that family background has a powerful effect on student performance (see, for example, Coleman et al. (1966) or Hanushek (1992)). If this factor is omitted from the statistical analysis, the estimates of pupil-teacher ratios can no longer be interpreted as the effect that class size might have on student performance. These estimates will be biased if there is any correlation across states between family backgrounds, such as income and education, and the average teacher-pupil ratio in the state. Considering estimates that do not take varying family backgrounds into account is a very significant quality problem, because estimates of the effect of variations in pupil-teacher ratios will then reflect family background and will appear to be important even when pupil-teacher ratios have *no* impact on student performance. Such an omission almost certainly leads to larger distortions than does considering estimates that do not consider the state policy environment.

In fact, Card and Krueger (1992b) was mistakenly included in the tabulations. Discussions with Krueger about the coding of the full set of estimates made it clear that this publication failed to take any aspect of family background into account, so it cannot adequately distinguish school effects from family effects on learning. The concern, as discussed above, is that family background and pupil-teacher ratios tend to be correlated, so that — if family background is omitted from the analysis — the estimated effect of the pupil-teacher ratio will not indicate the causal impact of differing pupil-teacher ratios but instead will just be a proxy for family background. While the analysis in Card and Krueger (1992b) stratifies by race or allows for a difference in the overall level of performance by race (i.e., an intercept dummy variable), the estimated effects for pupil-teacher ratio come from variations across states and over time in class size, when race is not observed to vary.[13] In other words, they treat all white and all black students as identical except for differences in class size or possibly other school attributes. Similarly, Card and Krueger (1992a) estimates models just for white males, and Krueger asserts that this is the same as the stratification by race in Link and Mulligan (1991). Link and Mulligan (1991), however, estimate value-added models that incorporate differences in family effects implicitly in the measures of prior achievement. Their estimates also include the racial composition of classrooms in their analysis, thus allowing them to sort out family background differences of classrooms from class size differences in a way that simple stratification does not. Given their analysis, there is no way to conclude that the Card and Krueger estimates of the pupil-teacher ratio are anything more than simply an indication of the omitted family background differences on student outcomes.

Finally, the Card and Krueger (1992a) analysis suffers not only from the biases of aggregate, cross-state analysis discussed previously but also from another set of fundamental shortcomings. The authors estimate state differences in the value of additional years of schooling according to 1980 Census information on labor market earnings and the state where workers were born (assumed to proxy where they were educated). They then relate the estimated value of a year of schooling to characteristics of the average school resources in the state in the years when a worker of a given age would have attended school. As critiques by Speakman and Welch (1995) and Heckman, Layne-Farrar, and Todd (1996a, 1996b) show, their estimates are very sensitive to the specific estimation procedures. First, the state earnings differences cannot be interpreted in terms of school quality differences in the way that Card and Krueger interpret them. In order to obtain their estimates of school quality, Card and Krueger (1992a) must assume that the migration of people across states is random and not based on differential earnings opportunities. Heckman, Layne-Farrar, and Todd (1996a, 1996b) show that there is selective migration and that this fundamental requirement for their interpretation is untrue. Second, they also show that the results differ significantly across time and that they are very sensitive to the precise specification of the models. Finally, Speakman and Welch (1995) further show that virtually all of the effects of state school resources work through earnings of college attendees, even though the resource measures relate only to elementary and secondary schools.

Statistical shortcomings such as these can be identified in other estimates, but this example illustrates why the mechanical re-weighting proposed by Krueger can in fact push the results in a biased direction. For Krueger's increased weightings to be appropriate, strong and quite implausible assumptions are necessary. Either variations in family factors and state policies must be irrelevant for student performance or, fortuitously, none of these factors prove to be correlated across states with average resources or pupil-teacher ratios.

Krueger's alternative weighting methods provide no better adjustments for anything that looks like quality of estimates. The two Card and Krueger articles are heavily cited in other articles, so that their combined weight increases to *17% of the total evidence* on a citation basis. But again this new weighting does not give an accurate estimate of the quality of the underlying estimates.[14] Similarly, the "selection-adjusted" weights place more emphasis on a positive and significant estimate if there was an estimated higher probability of getting a positive and significant estimate in an article (based solely on the number of estimates within each publication). The rationale behind this novel approach is entirely unclear and has no statistical basis.

Krueger seems to imply that he is making overall quality judgments in his tabulations when he selectively contrasts a few publications with both a large number of estimates and potentially damaging statistical problems with an analysis that has both a small number of estimates and better statistical modeling (Summers and Wolfe 1977). His mechanical tabulation approaches do not, however, provide such an overall quality assessment. The explicit quality considerations made in the bottom panel of Table 2-5 in fact eliminate all of the publications and estimates Krueger identifies as being problematic (i.e., the nine publications with eight or more estimates) — although they are eliminated on grounds of statistical quality and not because they simply provided too many separate estimates of class size effects. That panel also includes the Summers and Wolfe estimate, along with a number of other equally high-quality analyses of student achievement. But, most importantly, it also eliminates the 11 highly problematic estimates that come from estimates of the effect of pupil-teacher ratios using state-level analyses that ignore differences in the state policy environment.[15] These latter estimates have a disproportionate impact on each of his tabulations, even though they are arguably some of the poorest estimates of the effect of class size on student performance.

In sum, Krueger's reanalysis of the econometric evidence achieves

FIGURE 2D   Estimates for teacher-pupil ratio with alternative weighting

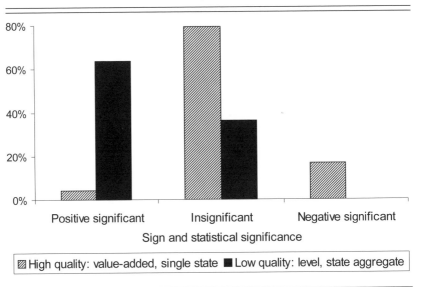

different results by emphasizing low-quality estimates. The low-quality estimates are demonstrably biased toward finding significant positive effects of class size reduction and of added spending. The differences in results for low- versus high-quality estimates is readily seen in **Figure 2-D**, which compares the pupil-teacher ratio estimates derived from state aggregate data with the class size estimates in the high-quality analyses identified in Table 2-5.

His discussion tries to suggest that one is caught on the horns of a dilemma: either weight heavily the estimates from the nine publications with the most estimates or weight heavily the low-quality state aggregate estimates. In reality, another option is available: weight neither heavily because both suffer from serious statistical problems. This option is exactly what is shown in the bottom of Table 2-5.

Remarkably, even when just re-weighted by the Krueger technique, the support of overall class size reduction policies remains weak. Most of the estimates, no matter how tabulated, are not statistically different from zero at conventional levels. Thus, even when heavily weighting low-quality estimates, he can achieve his rhetorical purpose of emphasizing that "class size is systematically related to student performance" only by giving equal weight to statistically insignificant and statistically significant results.

III. The Tennessee class size experiment (Project STAR)

A different form of evidence — that from random assignment experiments — has recently been widely circulated in the debates about class size reduction. Following the example of medicine, one large-scale experimental investigation in Tennessee in the mid-1980s (Project STAR) pursued the effectiveness of class size reductions. Random-assignment experiments in principle have considerable appeal. The underlying idea is that we can obtain valid evidence about the impact of a given well-defined treatment by randomly assigning subjects to treatment and control groups. This random assignment eliminates the possible contaminating effects of other factors and permits conceptually cleaner analysis of the outcomes of interest across these groups. The validity of any particular experiment nonetheless depends crucially on the implementation of the experiment. On this score, considerable uncertainty about the STAR results is introduced. But, ignoring any issues of uncertainty, the estimated impacts of large class size reductions are small and have limited application to the current policy proposals.

Project STAR was designed to begin with kindergarten students and to follow them for four years (Word et al. 1990). Three treatments were initially included: small classes (13-17 students); regular classes (22-25 students); and regular classes (22-25 students) with a teacher's aide. Schools were solicited for participation, with the stipulation that any school participating must be large enough to have at least one class in each treatment group. The initial sample included 6,324 kindergarten students. These were split between 1,900 in small classes and 4,424 in regular classes. (After the first year, the two separate regular class treatments were effectively combined, because there were no perceived differences in student performance).[16] The initial sample included 79 schools, although this subsequently fell to 75. The initial 326 teachers grew slightly to reflect the increased sample size in subsequent grades, although of course most teachers are new to the experiment at each new grade.

The results of the Project STAR experiment have been widely publicized. The simplest summary is that students in small classes performed significantly better than those in regular classes or regular classes with aides in kindergarten and that the achievement advantage of small classes remained constant through the third grade.[17]

This summary reflects the typical reporting, focusing on the differences in performance at each grade and concluding that small classes are better than large (e.g., Finn and Achilles 1990; Mosteller 1995). But it ignores the fact that one would expect the differences in performance to become wider through the grades because they continue to get more resources

FIGURE 2E   Expected vs. actual STAR results, Stanford Achievement Test, reading

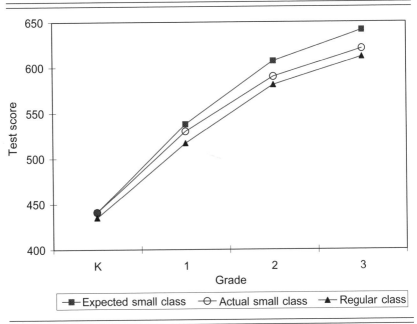

(smaller classes) and these resources should, according to the hypothesis, keep producing a growing advantage. **Figure 2-E** shows the difference in reading performance in small classes that was observed across grades in Project STAR. (The results for math performance are virtually identical in size and pattern). It also shows how the observed outcomes diverge from what would be expected if the impact in kindergarten were also obtained in later grades. As Krueger (1999) demonstrates, the small class advantage is almost exclusively obtained in the first year of being in a small class — suggesting that the advantages of small classes are not general across all grades.

The gains in performance from the experimental reduction in class size were relatively small (less than 0.2 standard deviations of test performance), especially in the context of the magnitude of the class size reduction (around eight students per class). Thus, even if Project STAR is taken at face value, it has relatively limited policy implications.

While the experimental approach has great appeal, the actual implementation in the case of Project STAR introduces uncertainty into these estimates (Hanushek 1999b). The uncertainty arises fundamentally from questions about the quality of the randomization in the experiment. In each year of the experiment, there was sizable attrition from the prior year's treatment groups, and these students were replaced with new students. Of the initial experimental group starting in kindergarten, 48% remained in the experiment for the entire four years.[18] No information, such as pretest scores, is available to assess the quality of student randomization for the initial experimental sample or for the subsequent additions to it. (The data in Figure 2-E are equally consistent with either a true small class advantage or an initial assignment of somewhat better students to small kindergartens). It is also impossible to assess adequately the impact of differential attrition of experimental subjects, particularly of those in larger classes disappointed over their placement. Substantial, non-random test taking occurs over the years of the experiment.

But, most important, the STAR results depend fundamentally on the choice of teachers. One measure of the importance of teachers relative to class size effects is that the average kindergarten achievement in small classes exceeds that in regular classes and regular-with-aide classes in only 40 of the 79 schools. While the teachers were to be randomly assigned to treatment groups, there is little description of how this was done. Nor is it easy to provide any reliable analysis of the teacher assignment, because only a few descriptors of teachers are found in the data and because there is little reason to believe that they adequately measure differences in teacher quality. The teacher data include race, gender, teaching experience, highest degree, and position on the Tennessee career ladder. While there is no information about the effect of career ladder position on student performance, none of the other measures has been found to be a reliable indicator of quality (Hanushek 1997).[19] Moreover, teachers all knew they were participating in an experiment that could potentially affect the future resources available from the state. The schools themselves were self-selected and are clearly not random. Small schools were excluded from the experiment, and all participating schools were willing to provide their own partial funding to cover the full costs. (This school selection issue is important, because the STAR experiment heavily oversampled urban and minority schools where the achievement response to the program is thought to be largest).[20] The net result of each of these effects is difficult to ascertain, but there is prima facie evidence that the total impact is to overstate the impact of reduced class size (Hanushek 1999b).

The STAR experiment is very important from a methodological perspective, a point emphasized in Hanushek et al. (1994), Mosteller (1995), and Krueger (1999, 2001). More random-assignment experimentation is desperately needed in schools. But the evidence from this specific experiment should be interpreted with caution. Mosteller (1995) makes a clear distinction between supporting the methodology of random assignment experimentation and ratifying the results from the single major experiment that currently exists.

Moreover, the evidence as it stands speaks just to the possible small effects of major and costly reductions in class size at kindergarten or first grade. It provides no evidence about beneficial effects at later grades. Nor does it indicate what effects could be expected from reductions of a smaller magnitude than the one-third reductions in Project STAR.

IV. Policy calculations

In addition to issues of how to interpret the existing class size evidence, Krueger (in chapter 1 of this volume) attempts to provide a justification for undertaking large class size reductions even if the effects are as small as currently estimated by Project STAR. His argument is simple: small effects on achievement may have large enough impacts on subsequent earnings that the policies are justified. In order to do these calculations, Krueger takes the perspective that the proper comparison is between doing nothing and undertaking large reductions in class size. This perspective is very narrow and would lead to quite wasteful policies. Moreover, even to get to this justification, he must make a number of heroic assumptions about achievement and the labor market. These assumptions imply enormous uncertainty in the calculations, and thus in the subsequent policy recommendations.

Krueger presents a series of calculations based on chaining together a variety of uncertain estimates about key aspects of the rewards to higher achievement. In order to obtain estimates of the labor market returns to class size reductions, one must multiply the effect of the class size reduction on achievement times the impact of early achievement differences on performance throughout schooling and into the labor market. The subsequent estimates of initial labor market advantage must be projected across a person's working life and then discounted back to kindergarten to compare to the costs of the original class size reduction. The uncertainty with each of those steps grows when they are compounded together. The relationship between early achievement and subsequent earnings, for example, relies on a single analysis of British labor market experiences for a group of individuals born in 1958; their wages were recorded in 1981 and 1991.[21] These estimates are employed to project what expected early career labor market experiences might be in the United States around 2015, the relevant period for the policy deliberations. While it may be academically interesting to see if there is any plausibility to the kinds of class size policies being discussed, one would clearly not want to commit the billions of dollars implied by the policies on the basis of these back-of-the-envelope calculations.[22]

Surely improving achievement of students is very important and should be the focus of policy attention. The issue is *not whether* society should invest in quality *but how* it should invest. Calculations that suggest the economic justification is as close to breakeven as found by Krueger do not make a good case for the huge commitment of resources implicitly behind his calculations — particularly when the uncertainty of the calculations is recognized.

The heart of the issue, however, is that Krueger ignores the fact that existing evidence points to other factors — particularly teacher quality — as being more important than class size. The extensive research on student achievement over the past 35 years has made it clear that there are very important differences among teachers. This finding, of course, does not surprise many parents who are well aware of quality differences of teachers, but it has eluded many researchers. Researchers have tended to confuse measurability of specific teacher characteristics related to quality with real differences in quality. That is, the econometric research has not identified any teacher attributes (such as education, experience, background, type of training, certification, or the like) that are highly related to the ability of some teachers to get particularly large or particularly small gains in student learning. Nonetheless, econometric analyses have identified large and persistent differences in the effectiveness of different teachers.[23]

The magnitude of differences in teacher quality is impressive. For example, looking at the range of quality for teachers within a single large urban district, teachers near the top of the quality distribution can get an entire year's worth of additional learning out of their students compared to those near the bottom (Hanushek 1992).[24] That is, a good teacher will get a gain of one-and-a-half grade level equivalents, while a bad teacher will get a half year for a single academic year. A second set of estimates comes from recent work on students in Texas (Rivkin, Hanushek, and Kain 2000). This analysis follows several entire cohorts of students and permits multiple observations of different classes with a given teacher. We look at just the variations in student performance that arise from differences in teacher quality within a typical school and do not consider any variations across schools. The variation in quality just within schools is large: moving from an average teacher to one at the 85th percentile of teacher quality (i.e., moving up one standard deviation in teacher quality) implies that the teacher's students would move up more than five percentile rankings in a single year.[25] These differences swamp any competing factors such as measured teacher and school attributes in their impact on student performance. For example, a one standard-deviation reduction in class size implies a 0.01-0.03 standard deviation improvement in student achievement. The lower-bound estimate on teacher quality summarized here implies that a one standard-deviation change in quality leads to a 0.12 standard-deviation increase in achievement. Finally, quality differences in teachers in Tennessee of a similar magnitude have also been estimated (Sanders and Horn 1995).

Recognizing the importance of teacher quality is central to the discussion of class size. First, any substantial reductions in class size imply hiring additional teachers. The success or failure of a class size reduction program will depend much more on whether the newly hired teachers are better or worse compared to the existing teachers than it will on the impact of class size reduction per se. In fact, depending upon the structure of the enabling legislation or policy, it could have quite detrimental effects. The 1996 class size reduction program in California, for example, left inner city schools scrambling for new teachers, partly as a result of suburban districts' bidding away experienced teachers (Stecher and Bornstedt 1999). The likely net result is that disadvantaged students — the hypothesized winners from the reduction policy — actually suffered a loss in educational quality. Second, the Krueger calculations never consider the possibility of much more attractive alternatives to either the current schools or to class size reductions. Employing higher-quality teachers could produce major impacts on student performance that are unachievable with any realistic or feasible class size reductions.

A major difference in policies aimed at class size reduction and those aimed at changing teacher quality is their relationship to incentives in schools. There is ample reason to believe that the current incentives related to student performance are too weak (Hanushek et al. 1994). Essentially nobody within schools has much riding on whether or not students achieve at a high level. The expected pay and career of a good teacher is about the same as that for a bad teacher. Class size reduction does nothing to change this. On the other hand, if schools are to move toward attracting and retaining higher-quality teachers, they will almost certainly have to build in stronger performance incentives for school personnel. The exact form that this would take is unclear, and discussion of the options is beyond the scope of this paper (see, however, Hanushek et al. 1994). The necessity of altering incentives on the other hand seems clear, at least to economists.

Reducing class size does not logically preclude doing other things, but it is almost certainly a practical deterrent. Limited political attention and constraints on public funds imply that strong moves toward class size reduction are almost certain to drive out better policies aimed at improving teacher quality. In fact, according to Krueger, locking in the current operations of schools would seem to be a natural and desirable result of pursuing class size reduction policies.

V. Conclusions

Despite the political popularity of overall class size reduction, the scientific support of such policies is weak to nonexistent. The existing evidence suggests that any effects of overall class size reduction policies will be small and very expensive. A number of investigations appear to show some effect of class size on achievement for specific groups or circumstances, but the estimated effects are invariably small and insufficient to support any broad reduction policies. Krueger's flawed analysis does little to contribute to the debate on technical grounds and, more importantly, cannot change the inherent costs and expected benefits of the basic policy. The re-analysis of econometric estimates relies on placing heavy weight on lower-quality and biased econometric estimates. Even then, the efficacy of class size reduction is in doubt. The majority of his re-weighted estimates are still statistically insignificant, i.e., we have relatively little confidence that there is any effect on student outcomes. The most optimistic estimates suggest that the policy effects on student achievement would be small. Krueger shows the policy effects to make sense given the cost only if one makes a number of strong but uncertain assumptions and only if one believes that no other school policy is feasible.

Proposed class size reduction policies generally leave no room for localities to decide when and where reductions would be beneficial or detrimental. The existing evidence does not say that class size reductions are never worthwhile and that they should never be taken. It does say that uniform, across-the-board policies — such as those in the current policy debate — are unlikely to be effective. For example, the theoretical analysis of class size by Lazear (forthcoming) — highlighted for other reasons by Krueger — points to optimal policies when schools are trying to maximize student achievement. In this case, he shows that across-the-board reductions are never going to be the correct policy.

A significant problem is that there are few incentives that drive decisions toward ones that improve student performance. Most economists believe that incentives are key to results — whether in education or in other aspects of life. But schools are not organized in a way that they will decide to reduce class size in instances where it is beneficial for student performance and not in other instances where it would not affect performance. Without such performance incentives, simply adding more resources is unlikely to lead to improvements in student achievement. In this regard, education has made very little progress in spite of the large and continuing investment in specific programs and activities.

Class size reduction is best thought of as a political decision. Past evidence suggests that it is a very effective mechanism for gaining voter support, even if past evidence also suggests that it is a very ineffective educational policy.

Appendix: Issues with the econometric data

In his essay in chapter 1 of this volume, Krueger raises a number of questions about the underlying estimates included in the overall summaries. Several of them were discussed with Krueger in private correspondence but did not make it into the published version.

Three coding questions are raised. First, as mentioned above, earlier correspondence determined that I had reversed the sign on the four estimated teacher-pupil ratio effects in Montmarquette and Mahseredjian (1989) in my previous tabulations. I have corrected this in Table 2-2 above, but Krueger subsequently does not make this correction in his tables. Second, Link and Mulligan (1986) included an ambiguous reference about whether teacher-pupil ratio was included in all 24 equations in their paper or just 12. Specifically, they noted that class size — which was discussed extensively in the modeling section — was insignificant in the mathematics equations, but they did not repeat mention of class size when they subsequently discussed the reading equations. In private communication with them designed to clarify this issue and to bring the most information to bear on the analysis, they indicated it was included in all 24 — and this was communicated to Krueger. Third, Kiesling (1967) is a journal article that extracted results from Kiesling's thesis (Kiesling 1965), and the teacher-pupil ratio results came from his thesis. While this was noted in Hanushek (1986), it was not noted in Hanushek (1997), although it also was communicated to Krueger. (The omission of teacher-pupil ratio from the published article based on his thesis is a clear example of the publication bias discussed above. In this case it could be reliably avoided).

Endnotes

1.   Pupil-teacher ratios are not the same as class size because of the use of specialist teachers, differences between numbers of classes taken by students and numbers taught by teachers, and other reasons. Nonetheless, because class size and pupil-teacher ratios tend to move together over time (see Lewit and Baker 1997) and because Krueger disregards any such distinctions, these differences are not highlighted at this time. The subsequent discussion here returns to the issue of when this distinction is most important. See also Hanushek (1999a).

2.   The NAEP has shown larger changes over time in the scores for 9- and 13-year-olds, but this has not been translated into improved scores at the end of high school; see Hanushek (1998a) for further discussion.

3.   Writing scores are first available in 1984. The mid-1980s saw a narrowing of the racial gap in achievement, but this stopped by 1990 and cannot be readily attributed to overall resource patterns. Further discussion of the aggregate trends including the racial trends can be found in Hanushek (1999a, 2001).

4.   The analysis by Grissmer et al. (1994) attempts to aggregate these changes over time based on econometric estimates of how various family backgrounds affect achievement. This analysis indicates that the overall preparation of white students (based on family background factors) seems to have improved, while that of black students seems to have worsened. While considerable uncertainty surrounds the estimation approach, the analysis strongly suggests that changing backgrounds are not masking the effects of school resource increases. A critique of the methodology is found in Hanushek (1999a).

5.   These tabulations were corrected for the previous miscoding of one article (Montmarquette and Mahseredjian 1989) that was pointed out to me by Alan Krueger. Krueger's analysis and tables of estimation results, however, do not adjust for this miscoding. A description of the criteria for inclusion is found in Hanushek (1997) and is summarized by Krueger in his earlier section.

6.   His discussion leads to some confusion in nomenclature. For reasons sketched below, my previous analyses have referred to distinct estimates as "studies" even though more than one estimate might appear in a given publication. Krueger changed this language by instead referring to separate publications as studies. Here I will generally drop the term studies and use the nomenclature of separate estimates in each publication.

7.   In some of the published articles, an element of ambiguity about the exact estimation procedures and results exists. In tabulating sample sizes, for example, it was not clear whether the estimation in Harnisch (1987) was conducted at the individual student or the school level. Calculating its sample size on the basis of schools would increase the correlation between sample size and number of estimates in each publication to 0.10 and would provide a slightly different distribution of sample sizes in Table 2-3. While these changes are inconsequential for this discussion, more consequential ambiguities, such as those noted by Krueger in his earlier section and in the appendix, also exist. At times it was possible to resolve the ambiguities by bringing in outside information, which seemed to be the appropriate way to extract the most information from the existing publications.

8.   The condition of unknown sign in the estimates makes it impossible to know how to include them in the simple calculation of signs of the estimates. His analysis assumes that there is no information in analyses that drop further consideration of pupil-teacher ratios after an initial investigation.

9.   This graph plots the Krueger results that do not correct the coding of Montmarquette and Mahseredjian (1989).

10.   Hanushek, Rivkin, and Taylor (1996) demonstrate that any bias in the estimated parameters will be exacerbated by aggregation of the estimation sample. For example, 11 of the 277 estimates of the effects of teacher-pupil ratios come from highly aggregated performance and resource data measured at the state level, the level of measurement where policy information is omitted from the analyses.

11.   Expenditure analyses virtually never direct analysis at performance across different classrooms or schools, since expenditure data are typically available only at the district level. Thus, they begin at a more aggregated level than many investigations of real resources.

12.   In fact, using aggregate state data frequently precludes any consideration of different effects by student background, subject matter, or what have you — offering an explanation for why these publications have just one estimate.

13.   Other estimates rely on race to measure family background characteristics, but they consider the racial composition of observed schools or classrooms. Even though it is not ideal, because parental education and income and other family attributes vary by race, including racial composition with measures of pupil-teacher ratios in these analyses can begin to sort out causation from correlation in ways that Card and Krueger (1992b) cannot. The prior analysis of high-quality analyses eliminates all such estimates.

14.   Card and Krueger (1992a) is rightfully cited for its innovative combination of labor market data with school quality data. However, because it has been controversial, it is cited in other works (such as Heckman, Layne-Farrar, and Todd 1996a, 1996b) without providing any endorsement for its quality. A large number of citations are also of two different types. The first is its use in introductory material to justify a new set of estimates, as in: "while the common view is that resources do not matter, Card and Krueger find that they do." The second use is by other researchers who are looking to justify use of expenditure data in a different kind of analysis, say of school choice or school spending patterns. Neither is a statement about quality relative to other articles.

15.   Krueger's discussion of Summers and Wolfe (1977) questions why just the estimate from individual student data is used instead of the estimate derived from aggregating the data to the school level. Of course, the aggregate school estimate will not be independent of the estimate from the individual data and, in this case, should be virtually identical except for issues of how precisely the effects are estimated. He does go further, however, to suggest that their school-level estimates provide a justification for using aggregate state data, because their estimates show larger class size effects when estimated with more aggregated data. Krueger, however, glosses over the most important issue about the quality of the state-level estimates: these estimates are misspecified because they ignore state policy differences, and the bias introduced by this problem is made worse by aggregating the data to the state level. No similar biases in the estimation of class size effects for data at the school level are apparent in Summers and Wolfe

(1977), and thus their aggregate estimates would not be subject to the quality problems of the state-level estimates.

16.   Surprisingly, policy discussions seldom focus on this finding about the ineffectiveness of teacher's aides. Indeed, the use of aides has grown dramatically since the time of the STAR experiment.

17.   Some students entered small classes in later grades, and their achievement was observed to be higher during their initial year of being in a small class than that of those in regular classes. See Hanushek (1999b) and Krueger (1999).

18.   Throughout the four years of the experiment there was also substantial and non-random treatment group crossover (about 10% of the small class treatment group in grades 1-3). That is, some students originally assigned to large classes moved to small classes later in the experiment. A smaller number also went in the opposite direction. These students were clearly not random. While this problem can be dealt with analytically, it lowers the information that can be obtained from the experiment.

19.   Further estimates of the magnitude of variation in teacher quality are provided below.

20.   Krueger (1999) identifies significantly stronger effects for disadvantaged students, and these effects will then be overweighted in calculating program average treatment effects.

21.   His discussion relies on the estimates in Currie and Thomas (1999). It also considers two alternative estimates, although they appear to differ substantially from the estimates chosen for the calculations. The unpublished estimates in Currie and Thomas (1999) have been subsequently modified in Currie and Thomas (2000), including the elimination of the joint estimation of different early tests on later outcomes. The implications of their revised estimates for Krueger's calculations are unknown.

22.   In his essay in chapter 1, Krueger suggests that, because of uncertainty, it might be appropriate to compare his calculated rate of return to class size reductions to a somewhat higher interest rate than the 4% he appears to favor. His suggestion of perhaps considering a 6% return, however, vastly understates the uncertainty one would calculate by the normal procedure of developing confidence intervals for the estimates that enter into his illustrative benefit-cost approximations.

23.   The econometric analysis behind these estimates involves calculating the average achievement gains across classrooms after allowing for differing student preparation, family background, and other factors. Some teachers consistently obtain high growth in student achievement, while others consistently obtain low growth. But standard measures of teacher characteristics are not correlated with quality as measured in terms of value-added to student performance.

24.   These estimates consider value-added models with family and school inputs. The sample includes only low-income minority students, whose average achievement in primary school is below the national average. The comparisons given compare teachers at the fifth percentile with those at the 95th percentile.

25.   For a variety of reasons, these are lower-bound estimates of variations in teacher quality. Any variations in quality across schools would add to this. Moreover, the estimates rely on a series of conservative assumptions that all tend to lead to understatement of the systematic teacher differences.

CHAPTER 3

A response to Eric Hanushek's "Evidence, politics, and the class size debate"

ALAN KRUEGER

In his comment in this volume, Eric Hanushek mischaracterizes my paper. My paper is not an attempt "to provide a justification for undertaking large class size reductions even if the effects are as small as currently estimated by Project STAR." Instead, I argue that, based on the data Hanushek assembled and the wider literature, "one should be reluctant to conclude that school resources are irrelevant to student outcomes." The central point of my paper is that Hanushek's conclusion that "the overall evidence provides little reason to believe that a general policy of class size reduction would improve student performance" does not hold up when sensible weights are used to combine the underlying studies in the literature, or when Hanushek's interpretation of many of the underlying studies is held up to close scrutiny. To the contrary, one can make a strong argument that the overall evidence provides little reason to believe that a general policy of class size reduction *would not* improve student performance, especially for minority and disadvantaged students. Moreover, the best-designed study available, the Tennessee STAR experiment, suggests that smaller class sizes have lasting benefits for the average student. To put those benefits in context, my paper offers a conservative cost-benefit analysis, the results of which suggest that, on the margin, an extra dollar spent to reduce class size raises students' future earnings by two dollars in present value.

At one level, Hanushek apparently now accepts a central theme of my reanalysis of his earlier literature surveys: that the quality of a study should be taken into account when summarizing the literature. We have different views of what constitutes a high-quality study, however. Hanushek has consistently assigned weights to studies in proportion to the number of estimates he extracted from them. He did so initially because each estimate was treated as a separate study. He continues to defend this practice, now arguing that studies from which he extracted more estimates are of higher quality, and he in turn argues that this justifies his original procedure. He even employs this uneven weighting scheme when he limits the sample to so-called "value-added studies," which he considers to be of particularly high quality.

The number of estimates Hanushek has taken from a study is a poor measure of the study's quality. First, all else equal, if a study carves up a given sample into smaller subsamples, it will have noisier estimates. Hanushek argues this is not the case in his sample, but he fails to hold constant the level of aggregation of the data underlying the study. For a given sample size, studies that use school-level data will yield noisier estimates than those that use district-level data because more of the idiosyncratic variability in achievement will be averaged out at a higher level of aggregation. Therefore, it is important to look at the relationship between sample size and the number of estimates extracted *for studies that use a common level of aggregation.* For example, among studies that use school-level data – the largest group of estimates in Hanushek's sample – there is a statistically significant, inverse correlation between the number of estimates Hanushek extracted and sample size. The median sample size was 878 for school-level studies from which only one estimate was extracted, 848 for such studies from which between one and seven estimates were extracted, and only 98 for such studies from which eight or more estimates were selected.[1]

Second, the refereeing process could generate an inverse correlation between the number of estimates a study reports and the quality of the study. I am pleased that Hanushek was persuaded by the analysis in my paper with David Card, which suggested that studies that reported an expected, statistically significant adverse effect of the minimum wage were more likely to be published in the early literature. But this argument has nothing to do with the *number* of estimates in a particular study. In fact, the Card and Krueger (1995) study that Hanushek cites used data from Brown et al.'s (1982) summary of the minimum wage literature. But Brown et al. extracted only one estimate per paper. Had Hanushek done likewise, his summary of the literature would have reached a different conclusion. The refereeing process outlined in my current paper is perfectly consistent with the one in Card and Krueger (1995). Authors who find an expected result are more likely to stop there in terms of what they report in their paper. Giving more weight to studies that report more estimates will misrepresent the findings of the studies as a whole.

Third, and most importantly, Hanushek acknowledges that "judgment" must be exercised in deciding which, and how many, estimates to select from a paper. A great deal of this judgment is open to question. One reason to give the studies equal weight is that the discretion of the researcher in selecting many estimates from some papers and few from others is limited if the studies are given equal weights.

Here are some examples of the questionable discretion that was exercised in selecting estimates:

- The Link and Mulligan (1991) study included no controls for family background variables, although it did estimate separate models for black, white, and Hispanic students. Evidently, this was considered a sufficient family background control to justify the extraction of 24 estimates in this case.[2] Also, percent minority was the only family background variable in Sengupta and Sfeir (1986). Card and Krueger (1992a, b), however, reported several distinct estimates of class size effects in separate samples of white and black males, but only one estimate was selected from each paper — and Hanushek now argues that it was a mistake to take any estimate from Card and Krueger (1992b).[3] By looking separately at blacks and whites, Card and Krueger's estimates control for race in a more flexible way than Sengupta and Sfeir, and probably absorb many unobserved family background variables by including state fixed effects.

- Twenty-four estimates of unknown sign were selected from Link and Mulligan (1986), although the text makes reference only to 12 estimates. In an email correspondence to me that Hanushek paraphrases in the appendix to his comment, he explained that "Link and Mulligan (1986) included an ambiguous footnote about whether teacher-pupil ratio was included in all 24 equations in their paper or just 12," which prompted him to contact Link and Mulligan and inquire about their unpublished estimates. This explanation is puzzling, however, because none of the four footnotes in Link and Mulligan (1986) concerns class size, and their text is quite clear that the reference to class size refers to their 12 math equations. (Because Link and Mulligan had quite small samples, it is not surprising that their results would be insignificant.) In any event, this example demonstrates that discretion was used in including some unpublished estimates.

- In some cases, Hanushek deviated from his stated rule of limiting studies to "a set of published results" by taking estimates from unpublished work, such as Kiesling's unpublished dissertation and Heim and Perl's (1974) Cornell working paper. In the case of Kiesling (1967), Hanushek now defends this practice as a way of preventing "publication bias" because studies with negative results may be less likely to be published. But no attempt was made to systematically gather estimates from other unpublished research.

- Hanushek classified Smith (1972) as having six estimates of unknown sign, yet I could find no reference to estimates of the effect of class size or the pupil-teacher ratio in Smith's paper. When I inquired, Hanushek provided the following rationale: "Mike reports reproducing the Coleman report results, showing that pupil-teacher ratios have no effect." While Smith reports having replicated "most" of the Coleman report results, he makes no specific reference to results concerning the pupil-teacher ratio. Moreover, Smith argues that his analysis puts "into question any findings at the secondary level about relationships between school resources and student achievement" from the Coleman report.

- Hanushek selected eight estimates from Sengupta and Sfeir (1986), which were all classified as negative. However, their estimates included a class size variable and an interaction between class size and the percent of students who are minorities. The interactions indicate that smaller classes have a beneficial effect on achievement at the average percent minority in the sample, but only the class size main effect is used. That is, the estimates Hanushek selected pertain just to whites. He ignored other estimates that were presented in the paper that dropped the interaction between race and class size; these showed a beneficial effect of smaller classes. Moreover, it is doubtful that the specifications used in the paper are sufficiently different to justify taking the eight estimates that Hanushek selected — half of the specifications differed only because a variable was added measuring non-teaching expenditure per student.

An agnostic approach is to give all studies equal weight, a common practice that limits the effect of researcher discretion. In his discussion of quantitative literature review methods, for example, T.D. Stanley (2000, 10) writes:

> A frequent problem occurs when more than one estimate (or test) of a desired effect is given in a study. When possible, we choose the estimate the author believes to be the best. Often, the multiplicity of estimates is generated through the use of different samples or countries. In order not

to give undue weight to a single study, one estimate should be chosen or averaged from many comparable estimates.

The fact that the equally weighted representation of the literature leads to a different conclusion than Hanushek's summary is disconcerting. Hanushek's summary of the literature does not accurately represent the findings of the studies that compose the literature, although it does represent the estimates he extracted from the studies. If the minority of studies that yielded the largest number of estimates are truly high-quality studies, then his representation of the effect of class size could be particularly informative. If not, however, I would argue that it is better to weight the studies equally, or by some commonly recognized measure of the quality of the study.

In general, the number of estimates a study reports is not likely to be related to the quality of the study. In fact, one could argue just the opposite. Suppose journals have a threshold quality level in order to publish a paper. A paper could pass that threshold by having a compelling analysis, or by presenting many estimates.[4] If this is the case, then quality and the number of estimates would be inversely correlated. The fact that the number of estimates of unknown sign rises with the number of estimates extracted suggests that study quality is not rising with the number of estimates taken. A careful study would report the sign of the main variables of interest.

Hanushek repeats his practice of placing more weight on studies from which he extracted more estimates even when he stratifies the sample on what he argues is a measure of quality in his results for so-called value-added studies (see his Figure 2D and Table 2-5). If the value-added studies were all of uniformly higher quality, why does he weight those studies from which he extracted more estimates more heavily?

In any event, all these results indicate is that most (fully 80%) of the value-added estimates that he extracted found insignificant effects of class size, probably because they have very small samples or use a limited range of variability in class size. They cannot reject a finding of no effect or, I suspect, a finding of an effect of the magnitude found in the STAR experiment in most cases. Indeed, most of these studies did not even report enough information to form confidence intervals to examine the precision of the estimates. A statistically insignificant finding does not necessarily mean that the results are inconsistent with class size having an effect – the effect may exist but the studies may lack sufficient power to detect it. Statistically insignificant estimates still yield information: they should be more likely to display a positive than negative effect of smaller class sizes if class size matters, even though the pattern would be noisy because of sampling variability. But Hanushek ignores that information and criticizes me for considering the sign of statistically insignificant estimates. He falls into the trap of arguing that the only good study is one with statistically significant results, ignoring the size of the coefficient, sample size, magnitude of the confidence intervals, other control variables, and so on.

It is disputable whether the 24 estimates that Hanushek refers to as "high quality" in Figure 2D and Table 2-5 are actually of high quality. Preliminarily, note that these 24 single-state, value-added estimates were drawn from just seven studies, with a median sample size of only 500 observations. In addition to yielding very noisy estimates, the quality of some of these studies for Hanushek's purposes is suspect. Kiesling (1984), for example, controlled for class size *and* the amount of large-group instruction, small-group instruction, and individualized instruction. This specification allows class size to vary, but not the amount of attention students receive from the teacher! Another study classified as a single-state, value-added study was based on data for pupils enrolled in Catholic schools in Montreal (an unusual definition of a state). This paper included class size and class size squared as separate variables. The six estimates traced out an inverted-shaped relationship between achievement and class size, with smaller classes estimated to have a beneficial effect for classes that were larger than average, and a negative effect for those that were smaller. Yet Hanushek classifies all six estimates as negative. Moreover, he codes three of them as statistically significant even though a joint F-test of the coefficients was not reported. Hanushek includes one estimate from Summers and Wolfe (1977) among these 24 estimates, but, as mentioned in my initial article, he failed to extract their estimate for low-achieving students, which revealed more beneficial effects of smaller classes.

These problems aside, there are good reasons to question whether the value-added studies are indeed of higher quality than the average study in the literature. The argument in favor of a value-added specification is that it helps to difference out omitted family and other variables: only the gain in that year is counted. But to overcome omitted variables the value-added specification must assume that family background and other omitted factors do not affect the *trajectory* of students once they enter school, or if they do that they are uncorrelated with class size. This assumption is preposterous. Children spend more time in the care of their families than they do in the care of schools. Moreover, the value-added specification ignores the impact of past school resources on current improvements in achievement: a good third grade class is presumed to have no affect on the strides a student makes in fourth grade. For these reasons, the biases that the value-added specification is intended to overcome could instead be exacerbated by such a specification. Indeed, Lindahl (2000) finds that the value-added specification leads to bias because it ignores the value that is added away from school during the summer. When he adjusts for this bias by subtracting summer-time changes in scores from year-over-year changes, he finds that class size has a beneficial effect on achievement.

The STAR experiment solves the omitted-variables problems without having to resort to the questionable assumptions underlying a value-added specification. Specifically, random assignment of students and teachers to class sizes breaks any connection between family background and other omitted factors and class size. For this reason, I think the STAR experiment provides the most compelling evidence presently available.

Indirect proxies of study quality are also available, such as the rank of a journal in which an article is published or the number of citations to an article. Hanushek objects to using article citation weights as a measure of quality because a particular study may be cited for reasons other than its quality. Fair enough. I have also calculated the tabulations using *journal citation* weights, that is, the average number of citations to all articles published in a journal. Surely there is consensus that the average paper published in the *American Economic Review* is of higher quality (and the review process more stringent) than the average paper published in the *Economics of Education Review* or in a non-peer-reviewed publication. Using journal citation figures as weights yields the same conclusion as the unweighted estimates.

A closer look at the nine studies
that receive the most weight

The debate over the quality of the studies on which Hanushek places most weight does not have to take place in a vacuum. What is the quality of the most heavily weighted studies in Hanushek's survey? Do they deserve a disproportionate amount of weight? **Table 3-1** summarizes the approach used and findings of the nine studies that account for 123 estimates in Hanushek's tabulations. Recall that class size is systematically related to student achievement in the remaining 50 studies in Hanushek's sample.[5] These nine studies, which overwhelmingly yield negative effects of smaller classes, are responsible for Hanushek's conclusion that there is no systematic relationship between class size and achievement. Moreover, if these studies are given the same weight as the others, the preponderance of the evidence in the literature points in the opposite direction of Hanushek's conclusion.

For a variety of reasons, many of the papers listed in Table 3-1 pro-

TABLE 3-1 Summary of the nine studies from which eight or more estimates were extracted

Study	Description
Burkhead (1967)	Stepwise regressions estimated using three school-level data sets. Chicago sample is 39 high-school-level observations; dependent variables are 11th grade IQ scores (proportion in stanine 5-9), 11th grade reading scores (proportion in stanine 5-9), residuals of reading and IQ scores from a regression on 9th grade IQ scores, high school dropout rate, and post-high school intentions; independent variables are teacher man-years per pupil, median family income, school enrollment, dropout rates, and eight other variables. Atlanta sample is 22 high-school-level observations; dependent variables are median 10th grade verbal achievement test score, residual of 10th grade verbal score from a regression on the 8th grade IQ score, male dropout rate, and percent enrolled in school year after graduation; independent variables include pupils per teacher, expenditures per pupil, teacher pay, median income, and four other variables. Sample of 176 high schools from Project Talent; dependent variables are average 12th grade r
Fowler and Walberg (1991)	Uses a backward stepwise regression procedure in which all explanatory varables are initially entered in the equation and then variables are dropped one by one until only the statistically significant ones remain. Eighteen dependent variables are used, ranging from math and reading tests to percent of students constructively employed, and 23 independent variables are used, including pupil-teacher ratio, expenditures per student, teacher salary, and school size. Sample consists of 199 to 276 N.J. high schools in 1985. Some variables are measured at the district level.
Jencks and Brown (1975)	Uses sample of students from 98 high schools from Project Talent data to estimate a two-step model. In first step, high school fixed effects are estimated from a regression that controls for students' 9th grade characteristics and test scores. In the second step, high school effects are related to class size, expenditures per student, and other school inputs, as well as mean post-high-school education plans in 9th grade and average SES. Sample size in second step estimation ranges from 49 to 95. Dependent variables are two measures of educational attainment (reported 15 months or 63 months after high school), career plans (by sex); occupation (by sex); and vocabulary, social studies, reading, and math tests.
Cohn and Millman (1975)	Sample consists of 53 Pennsylvania secondary schools from 1972. Eleven goals (test scores, citizenship, health habits, creative potential, etc.) are the outcome variables; exogenous explanatory variables are selected from 31 variables, including class size, instructional personnel per pupil, student-faculty ratio, and average daily attendance. Outputs are measured at 11th grade level, inputs are measured at the district, school, or 11th grade level. Stepwise regression is used to select the initial specifications; outcome variables were considered endogenous determinants of other outcomes if there was a high correlation between them and if "an a priori argument could support their inclusion in the model." Two-stage least squares, reduce form, and OLS estimates are reported. Instrumental variables are all excluded variables.

Hanushek coding of class size results	Comments
11 negative and insignificant, 3 positive and insignificant	It is unclear how the stepwise procedure was implemented. In many of the final models, none of the independent variables were statistically significant. More parameters are estimated than data points. Effects of pupil-teacher ratio, expenditures per pupil, and teacher pay are difficult to separately identify. IQ is supposed to be invariant to environmental factors, so it is an unusual outcome variable. Half of the class-size coefficients in the final models indicate a positive effect of smaller classes; it is unclear how Hanushek coded only three as positive. The average standardized effect size is a positive effect of smaller classes.
1 negative & significant, 1 positive and significant, 7 unknown and insignificant	Effect of pupil-teacher ratio is difficult to interpret conditional on expenditures per pupil. Pupil-teacher ratio is included in only four of the final 18 models reported. It is unclear how Hanushek selected nine estimates. Many of the dependent variables are highly related; for example, average math score, percent passing the math exam, and the percent passing both the math and reading exam are used as the dependent variable in separate equations, as are math and reading scores from the Minimum Basic Skills Test and High School Proficiency Test.
3 negative and significant, 3 negative and insignificant, 4 unknown and insignificant	The sample consists only of those who were continuously in high school between 9th and 12th grades. Thus, high school dropouts are truncated from the sample, so any effect of high school characteristics on high school dropout behavior, and related career implications, is missed. Based on the results in Table 9, the four estimates Hanushek classified as unknown signs all have positive effects of smaller classes on test scores.
1 negative and significant, 9 negative and insignificant, 1 positive and insignificant	Hanushek appears to have selected the OLS model results, which are the weakest for class size. The reduced form estimates indicate eight positive effects of smaller classes and three negative ones, all of which are insignficant. The simultaneous equation models indicate three positive and three negative coefficients, all of which are insignificant. Procedures to select exogenous explanatory variables, endogenous variables, and exclusion restrictions are open to question.

(continued)

TABLE 3-1 *(cont.)* **Summary of the nine studies from which eight or more estimates were extracted**

Study	Description
Link and Mulligan (1986)	Separate OLS regression models for math and reading scores were estimated for 3rd, 4th, 5th, and 6th graders, by white, black, and Hispanic background, yielding 24 regressions. Explanatory variables are pretest score, interaction between large class (26 or more) and majority-below-average classmates, dummy indicating whether teacher says student needs compensatory education, mother's education, weekly instructional hours, sex, teacher experience. Student is unit of observation. Sample drawn from Sustaining Effects dataset. Median sample size is 237 students.
Link and Mulligan (1991)	Separate OLS regression models for math and reading scores were estimated for 3rd, 4th, 5th, and 6th graders, by white, black, and Hispanic background, yielding 24 regressions. Explanatory variables are pretest score, class size, a dummy indicating whether teacher says student needs compensatory education, weekly instructional hours, sex, same race percentage of classmates, racial busing percentage, mean pre-test score of classmates, standard deviation of pre-test score of classmates. Student is unit of observation. Sample drawn from Sustaining Effects dataset. Median sample size is 3,300.
Maynard and Crawford (1976)	Study designed to look at effect of family income on children's outcomes. Data from Rural Income Maintenance Experiment in IA and NC. Dependent variables are days absent (grade 2-9 or 9-12), comportment grade point average, academic GPA (grade 2-9 or 9-12), and standardized achievement tests (deviation from grade equivalents scores or percentile ranks). More than 50 explanatory variables, including expenditures per student (IA), enrollment, log enrollment per teacher, income, log average daily attendance relative to enrollments, average test score for student's grade and school (NC), remedial program, etc. Student is unit of observation. Estimates equations separately for each state.
Sengupta and Sfeir (1986)	Sample contains 50 or 25 school-level observations on 6th graders in California. Dependent variables are math, reading, writing, and spelling test scores. Explanatory variables are average teacher salary, average class size, percent minority, and interaction between percent minority and class size. Another set of four models also controls for non-teaching expenditures per pupil. Estimates translog production functions by LAD.
Stern (1989)	Uses school-level data from California to regress test scores on average student characteristics, teachers per student, the square root of the number of students, and teacher pay. Math, reading, and writing tests are used in two school years, yielding 12 estimates. Median sample size is 2,360 students.

Hanushek coding of class size results	Comments
24 unknown and insignificant	Models reported include interaction between large class size and peer effects but not class size main effect. The text states that when class size was included as a main effect in the math equations it was not individually statistically significant; no joint test of the class-size-peer-group interaction and main effect is reported. The interactions generally indicate that students with weak peers do better in smaller classes. No mention of the main effect of class size in the reading equations is reported, so it is unclear how Hanushek could classify 24 estimates as insignificant. The class-size-peer-group interactions generally indicate that students in classes with low achievers do better in smaller classes.
3 negative & significant, 8 negative and insignificant, 5 positive and significant, 8 positive and insignificant	No family background variables except race. Standard errors do not correct for correlated effects within classes. Compensatory education variable is potentially endogenous.
2 negative & significant, 3 negative and insignificant, 2 positive and significant, 4 positive and insignificant	Class size is just an ancillary variable in a kitchen-sink regression designed to look at the effect of random assignment to an income maintenance plan. Class size effects are difficult to interpret once expenditure per student is held constant. Many of the explanatory variables (e.g., average class performance and attendance relative to enrollment) further cloud interpretation of class size effects.
7 negative and significant, 1 negative and insignificant	No controls for family background other than percent minority. It is unclear why the specifications are sufficiently different to justify taking eight as opposed to four estimates. In all eight equations, interactions between class size and percent minority indicate that smaller classes have a beneficial effect at the average percent minority, but only the class size main effect is used.
9 negative and significant, 3 positive and insignificant	The nine equations that yield negative effects of teachers per student in a grade level also control for the number of students in the grade level; the three positive estimates exclude this variable. More students in a grade level have a strong, adverse effect on scores. If the teacher-pupil ratio has a nonlinear effect, the number of students in a grade level could be picking it up. In addition, variability in class size in this paper is not due to shocks in enrollment, which many analysts try to use in estimating class size effects.

vide less than compelling evidence on class size effects. Yet Hanushek's argument requires that these studies contain the strongest evidence. Consider some of the following problems encountered in using these studies for this purpose:

- One-third of the studies estimated regression models that included expenditures per pupil and teachers per pupil as separate variables in the same equation. Sometimes this was the case because stepwise regressions were estimated (e.g., Fowler and Walberg 1991), and other times it was a deliberate specification choice (e.g., Maynard and Crawford 1976). In either case, the interpretation of the class size variable in these equations is problematic. For a school to have a lower pupil-teacher ratio but the same expenditures per student, it must skimp on something else.

- Jencks and Brown (1975) analyze the effect of high school characteristics on students' educational attainment, but their sample is necessarily restricted to individuals who were continuously enrolled in high school between 9th and 12th grade. Thus, this sample misses any effect of class size on high school dropout behavior — a key determinant of educational attainment. Moreover, although Hanushek coded four of their estimates as having unknown signs, the coefficients are available from another table.

- Fowler and Walberg (1991) estimate several models using the same sample of observations but many different outcome variables. The outcome variables are highly related, such as the average math score and the percent passing the math exam.

- Hanushek selected 11 OLS estimates from Cohn and Millman (1975), but he excluded estimates that corrected for simultaneity bias. The latter estimates were consistently more positive and were the authors' preferred estimates. The OLS estimates that Hanushek selected controlled for both the average class size in a high school and the pupil-teacher ratio, a clear specification error.

My review of the studies in Table 3-1 is not meant as a criticism of the contributions of these studies. Many are excellent studies. But problems arise in Hanushek's use of the estimates he extracted from these studies because, in many cases, the authors designed the studies not to examine the effect of class size per se, but rather to look at some other feature of the education process. Maynard and Crawford, for example, were interested in the effect of exogenous shifts in family income (arising from the Rural Income Maintenance Experiment) on children's academic outcomes, and the study provides persuasive results on this issue; class size and expenditures per pupil were just ancillary variables that the researchers held constant. Indeed, some of the authors (e.g., Jencks and Brown) cautioned against interpreting their class size variables because of weaknesses in their data or analysis. Yet Hanushek gives them much more weight than the average study.

After looking at the description of the studies in Table 3-1, can anyone seriously believe Hanushek's argument that, "The typical publication with several estimates actually provides more evidence than would be the case if only one estimate per publication were reported"? Moreover, the typical study from which Hanushek extracted multiple estimates often did not contain more estimates than studies from which he extracted only one estimate, even using his criterion of what constitutes a separate estimate. It is hard to argue that these nine studies deserve 123 times as much weight as Summers and Wolfe's (1977) *American Economic Review* article, for example. Indeed, given the considerable discretion used to select the estimates, it would seem to be a much more sensible and fair description of the literature to put equal weight on all the studies than to weight them by the number of estimates Hanushek extracted.

Hanushek argues that aggregate-level estimates in Summers and Wolfe are biased by omitted state-level variables. That is, he maintains that the very same states that in his view waste money on school resources like smaller classes have another set of policies that improve student achievement, creating a bias in the state-level analyses. He does not specify what such policies might be, however. Moreover, he provides no evidence of their existence. This problem, which at best should be regarded as highly speculative, seems trivial compared to the statistical problems in the nine studies from which Hanushek extracted 123 estimates, and which must be given excessive weight to support his conclusion that smaller class sizes would not help the average student.

Statistical significance of estimates

Hanushek emphasizes that, no matter how weighted, most of the estimates he extracted from the literature are statistically insignificantly different from zero. This should not be a cause of solace for him, however, since such a result is not surprising given the small sample sizes used in most of the literature. By Hanushek's count, the median sample size used in estimates in the literature is 385 observations (accordingly, half were

FIGURE 3A   95% confidence interval, actual STAR data and if STAR sample size equaled Hanushek's median sample size

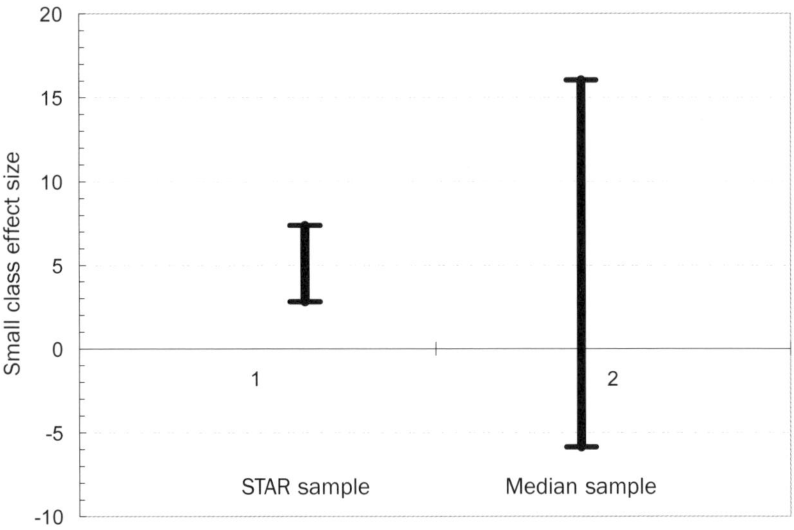

Note: Effect size is measured in percentile points.

smaller). The sample size in the STAR experiment was around 6,000 per grade.

Figure 3A illustrates the effect of sample size on the precision of the estimated class size effect. It shows a 95% confidence interval for the effect of a seven-student reduction in class size for third graders from the STAR experiment. The scores are measured in percentile units. Every point contained within the confidence interval would *not* be rejected if it were the null hypothesis. Importantly, zero is not covered by the confidence interval, which is why class size had a statistically significant effect in this sample.

Had the sample size in the STAR experiment been 385 — the median for the estimates in Hanushek's sample — the estimated confidence interval would have been 4.5 times wider, and would have contained zero. The expected t-ratio would be less than 1.0 if the STAR sample size were as small as that used in the median estimate in the literature. Hence, an effect of the magnitude found in the STAR experiment would have been indistinguishable from zero in most of the estimates in Hanushek's sample.

Given this result, it is not surprising that most of the estimates are statistically insignificant. For this reason, I have emphasized the fraction of

FIGURE 3B   Relationship between math and reading NAEP scores and pupil-teacher ratio, 17-year-olds, 1970-96

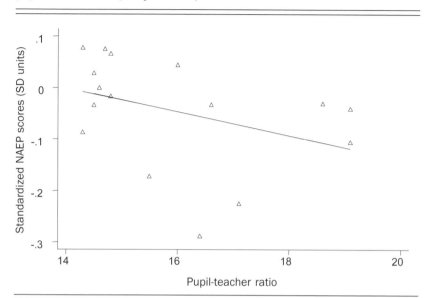

estimates that are positive relative to those that are negative. The problem is not that class size has an unimportant effect; rather, the problem is that the samples used to derive the estimates that Hanushek extracted are typically too small to detect an effect of reasonable magnitude.

NAEP data

Hanushek argues that the historical trends in school spending and aggregate test performance are not supportive of the view that smaller classes have helped students. Given his criticism of aggregate analysis, it is somewhat ironic that he relies on aggregate data for this argument.

Nonetheless, the aggregate data are not supportive of his view. The correlation between NAEP math and reading test scores for 17-year-olds and the contemporaneous pupil-teacher ratio is negative, as **Figure 3B** illustrates. Indeed, the slope of the relationship is almost exactly what one would have predicted from the STAR experiment. If science scores are included, the relationship becomes much weaker, but if scores for younger students are included it becomes much stronger.

More importantly, the careful, less aggregative analyses of the NAEP data that have been performed by Wenglinsky (1998) and Grissmer (2001) indicate that smaller pupil-teacher ratios are associated with higher student achievement.

Hanushek's comparison of SAT scores to the pupil-teacher ratio over time is also flawed. He makes no attempt to adjust for the increasing proportion of students who take the exam. When more students take the SAT exam, the average score falls, as the marginal students writing the exam tend to be weaker students. Card and Payne (1998), using state-level data, adjust for the share of students writing the SAT, and they find that increases in educational expenditures in response to court decisions requiring more equal spending are associated with increases in SAT scores.

Minor points of disagreement

- Hanushek accuses me of causing some confusion in nomenclature. He writes, "my previous analyses have referred to distinct estimates as 'studies' even though more than one estimate might appear in a given publication. Krueger changed this language by instead referring to separate publications as studies." This is an odd accusation. Hanushek (1986), for example, uses the word "study" in multiple ways within the same publication. The very first use of the word "study" in Hanushek (1986), for example, pertains to an entire publication. I have not changed the language; I just used one of Hanushek's multiple usages. Whatever confusion exists in the nomenclature — and I believe there is some because many researchers and journalists have misunderstood Hanushek when he used the word "study" to mean a separate estimate — certainly predates my paper.

- Hanushek asserts that the relationship between early achievement and subsequent earnings used in my cost-benefit analysis "relies on a single study of British labor market experiences." This is inaccurate: I discussed studies of U.S. data as well as British data in my paper. The economic return from smaller classes is somewhat larger if the U.S. studies are used for this calculation.

- Hanushek claims, "Krueger suggests that the publication of multiple estimates is largely whimsical and misguided, the reality is that there are generally sound econometric reasons behind many of these decisions." I suggest no such thing. What I would suggest is whimsical and misguided is Hanushek's use of the multiple estimates in his summary of the articles in the literature, not the researchers' presentation of the estimates. Sometimes Hanushek takes estimates when none are presented; other times he takes estimates that are not the authors' preferred ones. Moreover, there is no reason to believe there is more information in a study that presents many estimates of a bad specification than in a study that presents one estimate of a good specification.

- Hanushek argues that, "If there are different effects [of class size] for different subsamples of students, providing a single estimate across the subsamples...is incorrect from a statistical point of view and would lead to biased results." As a statistical matter, this is incorrect. If there are heterogeneous treatment effects, they can be averaged. Reducing class size in the STAR experiment did not raise achievement in all schools, but the schools can be pooled together and one overall average effect estimated. For many public policy purposes, one is interested in the average effect. Presumably, this is why Hanushek pools together estimates for different subsamples in his summary of the literature.

- Hanushek criticizes me for not correcting his miscoding of Montmarquette and Mahseredjian (1989), after I pointed out his coding error to him. As was conveyed to Hanushek, I did not correct his mistakes in my analysis "because I wanted to emphasize that the difference in our results was the weighting, not the coding of the studies." I believe he miscoded a number of other studies as well — for example, estimates were taken from an unpublished draft of Kiesling's paper, in violation of the stated selection rule — and I didn't change these other miscodings to emphasize that the weighting scheme generated the different results, not the more accurate coding of estimates. It might be a good exercise to comb through the entire literature and apply a consistent set of judgments to the way estimates are extracted and categorized, but that is not what I have tried to do here.

- Hanushek claims that, "The likely net result [of California's class size reduction initiative] is that disadvantaged students — the hypothesized winners from the reduction policy — actually suffered a loss in educational quality." The evidence does not support this conclusion. For example, Stecher and Bohrnstedt (2000) find that the gain in achievement on the math exam was 0.10 standard deviations larger in schools with 75% or more minority students compared to those with 25% or fewer minority students, but this differential effect was not statistically significant.

- Hanushek argues that Lazear's (2000) model implies that across-the-board class size reductions "are never going to be the correct policy." This is a consequence of assumed optimizing behavior on the part of schools in that model. Such behavior implies that *any* across-the-board policy change would not be optimal. A small across-the-board reduction in class size, however, would still generate close to a normal rate of return in this model. In any event, most policy considerations of class size reduction take place in the context of *targeted* reductions. Personally, I think a stronger case could be made for targeting class size reductions to disadvantaged children because they seem to benefit the most from such initiatives. For this reason, I think it is particularly harmful that Hanushek's literature summaries have frequently been used in school-equity court cases to argue against increasing resources for poor children. I also think it is unfortunate that he frequently ignored estimates for subsets of disadvantaged and minority students.

- Hanushek argues that teacher quality is more important than class size. I have no doubt that teacher quality is an important determinant of student success. But Hanushek offers no plan for improving teacher quality, and he provides no evidence that any policy intended to improve teacher quality results in a greater boost to achievement than class size reduction. Moreover, he has argued that improving teacher pay would not lead schools to recruit better teachers, contrary to standard economic logic. To the contrary, I suspect a major reason why his results (even with his skewed weights) indicate that greater expenditures per student lead to higher achievement is that teacher pay is a major source of school spending. I also suspect that a decline in teacher quality is one reason why the aggregate data that Hanushek cites do not show a larger improvement over time (see, e.g., Lakdawalla 2001 and Bacolod 2001).

- Hanushek unnecessarily politicizes serious research issues in arguing that "Class size reduction is best thought of as a political decision" and by asserting, "Before the political popularity to voters of reductions in class size became known, most educational researchers and policy makers had discarded such policies as both too expensive and generally ineffective." First, in a democracy, all education policy decisions are political, as they should be. Second, the only survey of educational researchers on the effect of class size that I am aware of finds that most believe that smaller classes are associated with improved performance. Hanushek offers no support for his representation of the views of educational researchers. Third, Hanushek's Figure 2-A indicates that the pupil-teacher ratio was declining throughout most of the post-war period, so it is obvious that such policies were not discarded by policy makers, as he alleges. Fourth, his own categorization of studies in the literature — not to mention more conventional and more persuasive meta-analyses — suggests that there is an ample research base to justify consideration by politicians, parents, educators, and researchers of class size reduction proposals.

Conclusion

Hanushek raises one final objection to my reanalysis of his literature summary that goes to the heart of this type of an exercise. He criticizes my equally weighted tabulations because "it is often impossible to combine the separate samples used for obtaining the individual estimates....There is no way in which [Burkhead et. al.'s distinct estimates] can be aggregated into a single estimate of the effect of class size." But what is Hanushek doing when he aggregates estimates from the entire literature? Isn't he combining disparate outcomes from the same study, and from different studies, to derive an overall estimate? Why is my sin of first aggregating within studies worse than his of aggregating the entire literature? The only difference is that Hanushek combines estimates in such a way as to give much more weight to some studies — the ones from which he extracted more estimates — than to others. My approach gives a quantitative impression of what the *publications* in the literature have found. Hanushek's approach of weighting the publications by the number of estimates he extracted from them gives a biased representation of what the publications have found.

Hanushek tries to justify his procedure by arguing that the majority of studies, from which he extracted relatively few estimates, are lower-quality studies because they tend to analyze aggregate data. But his contention that studies of more aggregate data yield estimates that are biased upward relative to those of disaggregate data is unconvincing, and certainly not proved. First, he asserts that unobserved state policies are correlated with school spending and student achievement. He never identifies these mysterious policies. What are they? What happens to the results if these X-variables are held constant? Moreover, if Hanushek is correct that the highest-quality studies show that spending more money to reduce class size yields a negative return, it is hard to imagine that states that so badly misuse their expenditures would have other policies in place that more than counteract this inefficient policy. Second, as James Heckman and others have argued, biases that cause researchers to estimate *too small* an effect of school resources in disaggregate data are also likely. For example, many states have compensatory education funding, which would cause schools with low-achieving students to receive additional resources. This type of phenomenon would cause school-level studies to estimate too small an effect of school resources, but is unlikely to affect state-level studies. Third, the STAR experiment is based on class-level class size data and uses random assignment to break any possible connection between class size and student background — and the STAR results suggest that smaller classes do have a beneficial effect. Fourth, the school resource data researchers use are commonly noisy measures of actual resources. Random measurement errors in school resource data would attenuate the estimated effect of those resources. By averaging data across students in a state or district, the effect of these measurement errors is reduced. As a consequence, measurement error bias is smaller in aggregate data.

Because of the conflicting biases that might arise in micro and aggregate data, Heckman, Layne-Farrar, and Todd (1996a, 287) argue that "Much more study of the political economy of school expenditure is required to understand the importance of this [Hanushek's aggregation bias] argument." Surely, it is premature to place much extra weight on the studies that report many estimates in the belief that these studies are higher quality because they tend to use disaggregate data.

It should be clear that Hanushek's interpretation of the literature rests entirely on his subjective interpretation of what constitutes a high-quality study. Based on the inspection of the studies that received the most weight in Hanushek's tabulation, I would question his implicit definition of "high quality."

Hanushek accuses me of "massaging" the econometric evidence. That is a strong charge.[6] I'll let the reader decide whether it is massaging the evidence to weight all studies equally or to assign 24 times as much weight to a study published in the *Economics of Education Review* (which did not even report estimates of the coefficient of interest) than to one published in the *American Economic Review*. Personally, I think the least-manipulatable way to quantitatively summarize the studies in the literature is to give each study equal weight.

Endnotes

1.   The correlation between the square root of the sample size and the number of estimates Hanushek extracted is -0.24 at the school level, 0.07 at the class level, -0.10 at the grade level, -0.34 at the district level, and -0.17 at the state level.

2.   In their first footnote, Link and Mulligan (1991) write: "We found, however, that [education of the mother, education of the father, number of books in the home, family income, home ownership, and rooms per family member] did not provide a systematic and consistent explanation for student achievement. These variables are not part of the larger sample used in the present study." Hanushek inserted another explanation for why he thinks Link and Mulligan controlled for family background in the revised draft of his comment: they "estimate value-added models that incorporate differences in family effects implicitly in the measures of prior achievement." This is a novel justification; but it also ignores the fact that Card and Krueger estimated models with state fixed effects, which control for unobserved family effects as well.

3.   Hanushek notes that Link and Mulligan (1991) included the average race of one's classmates, and argues that this sets it apart from Card and Krueger's (1992a and b) analysis. But this argument is misleading for two reasons. First, Card and Krueger (1992b) looked at black and white students who attended *segregated* schools, so racial composition of classmates was, in fact, held constant. Second, racial composition is not a measure of students' family background. (The latter argument did not seem to prevent him from taking eight estimates from Sengupta and Sfeir.) I'm not arguing that Link and Mulligan (1991) should be excluded, only that Hanushek has employed a varying definition of family background to extract estimates.

4.   See Ellison (2000) for a q-r theory of publication standards.

5.   The 154 estimates in the remaining 50 studies are twice as likely to be positive as negative.

6.   Hanushek's overheated rhetoric brings to mind John Kenneth Galbraith's (1955) classic observation: "Although a vehement argument may mean that an important question is being decided, it far more frequently means only that a hopelessly outnumbered minority is making itself felt in the only way it can."

CHAPTER 4

Making the evidence matter: Implications of the class size research debate for policy makers

JENNIFER KING RICE

Considerable disagreement has characterized exchanges among researchers interested in a better understanding of the impact of various types of investments in public education in the U.S. This controversy, often referred to as the "does money matter?" debate, has been fueled in large part by a series of literature reviews by Hanushek (1981, 1986, 1996a, 1997) that have shown a high level of inconsistent and insignificant findings across studies estimating the impact of different types of educational investments. Researchers who have reanalyzed Hanushek's data, challenging both his assumptions and his basic "vote counting" methodology, have reported more positive and consistent interpretations of the same set of studies. In their reanalysis, Hedges, Laine, and Greenwald (1994) drew on several statistical methods in meta-analysis and found a systematic relationship between educational inputs and outcomes large enough to be of "practical importance." Further, Laine, Greenwald, and Hedges (1996), assembling and analyzing a new universe of production function studies, concluded that school resources are systematically related to student performance and that the magnitudes of the relationships are again large enough to warrant attention. In addition, Krueger's reanalysis included in this volume focuses on publications rather than on individual estimates (essentially altering the weights that Hanushek's analysis assigns to studies) and finds the effect of educational investments on student achievement to be more positive, consistent, and significant than Hanushek had found.

Class size is one component of this broader debate. Hanushek (1997) reviewed 227 estimates of the impact of teacher-pupil ratio on student performance and reported 15% as significant and positive, 13% as significant and negative, and 72% as statistically insignificant. Krueger's reanalysis that weights each publication equally reports 26% of the studies to be significant and positive, 10% significant and negative, and 64% statistically insignificant. Using alternative weights, Krueger finds even greater evidence supporting positive and statistically significant findings of the impact of class size on student performance. So, although research on the impact of class size has been conducted, the literature offers little closure or clear direction for policy makers considering investments in smaller classes.

While divergent interpretations of the same evidence are both acceptable and potentially productive in the research community, if research is to inform practice, we must work toward some agreement about what the research does and does not tell us, and what it can and cannot tell us. The type of exchange between Krueger and Hanushek presented in this volume is potentially fruitful. Given the great deal of attention that the issue of class size is receiving in both research and policy circles, efforts like these to make sense of the existing evidence hold great potential and can be valuable.

This essay emphasizes the policy implications of the class size literature and the debate surrounding it. The discussion begins by considering the nature of the debate itself, and then shifts to describe four interrelated observations from the literature that provide insight into the complexity of the reform for both policy makers and researchers. The conclusion provides four recommendations for future research that could help to shed greater light on this important issue.

The nature of the debate

While exchanges like the one between Krueger and Hanushek presented in this volume have the virtue of exposing the complexity of estimating the impact of education policies, they also have the potential to unwittingly suggest to policy makers and the broader public that the research community is incapable of drawing conclusions about major education policy alternatives. This perception can seriously undermine the role of education research in informing public policy debates, and its accuracy should be questioned. Class size reduction policies have become a popularly supported education reform alternative, and evidence of the growing public support for smaller classes is not hard to find. It seems as though policy makers, frustrated with the lack of agreement in the research community, are side-stepping the gridlock and are moving forward with the implementation of class size reduction policies, often without the benefit of research to guide their efforts. However, research can and should play a role in these decisions. Researchers perhaps need to refocus their efforts to address the rigor of the research as well as the relevance of the conclusions to those who make policy decisions. In other words, while we need to continue to expose and sort out how the same evidence can lead to dramatically different conclusions, we also need to try to identify points of agreement so that research can make a productive contribution to the policy process.

So, it seems a reasonable place to begin is with points of consensus. Perhaps the most important of these is that both Hanushek and Krueger seem to agree that smaller class size *can* matter in *some* circumstances. A number of explanations have been advanced to account for the inconsistencies among the many non-experimental studies that have estimated the impact of class size. These include poor measures of key variables (e.g., class size versus student-teacher ratio), model specification issues (levels of analysis, proper controls, interaction effects, non-linear relationships), and key assumptions underlying the studies (see Grissmer 1999). While continued efforts are being made to explain the conflicting results of the non-experimental studies, a more consistent set of findings is emerging from research on the impact of class size that is based on experimental or quasi-experimental designs. Analysis of the Project STAR experiment suggests that, depending on a variety of factors, the estimated effect of reducing classes by about seven students to 15-16 per class was as high as a third of a standard deviation (Finn and Achilles 1999). These effect sizes are not trivial, and comparable results were reported for the quasi-experimental study in Wisconsin, Project SAGE (Molnar et al. 1999). Both of these studies also provide some evidence that the effects are larger for students from minority and low-income families. Taken together, this body of research suggests increasingly persuasive evidence that reducing class size *can* be an effective policy choice.

The key to improving student achievement through this strategy lies in reaching a better understanding of several questions. For whom do smaller classes matter most? Under what circumstances? At what cost? Such knowledge is needed to move the policy community beyond questions of whether to reduce class sizes to questions of how to do it well, right, and most productively.

Policy issues

Four interrelated issues are arguably important for policy makers to consider as they think about making the substantial investments needed to reduce class sizes. All have implications for the cost-effectiveness of the policy and all give rise to directions for future research.

1.   *Targeted implementation* — Evidence from trend analysis, non-experimental studies, as well as experimental and quasi-experimental studies suggests that the positive effects of smaller classes are most pronounced for students from minority and low-income families (Finn and Achilles 1999; Molnar et al. 1999; Nye, Hedges, and Konstantopoulos 1999). Rather than implement universal class size reduction policies, targeting smaller classes to schools with higher concentrations of these types of students may produce the greatest return on the investment — the costs would presumably be lower and the effects higher. In addition to being more efficient, such targeted policies also have the potential to contribute to the equity and adequacy of students' education opportunities. Indeed, some researchers and many states have used class size as a defining characteristic of what counts as an adequate education (Clune 1994).

2.   *Adequate infrastructure* — In considering the adoption of any policy alternative, it is important to consider not just the direct costs associated with that intervention but also the kind of infrastructure that needs to be in place if the intervention is to work. A good example is the California Class Size Reduction program, which set out to reduce all classes in grade K-3 across the state to 20 students or fewer (see California Legislative Analyst's Office 1997). Over $1 billion was provided to support the hiring of new teachers, but a limited supply of two other important resources complicated implementation: (1) a large pool of qualified teachers to assume the new positions, and (2) adequate facilities to accommodate the dramatic increase in the number of classes (Bohrnstedt, Stecher, and Wiley 2000). Given what we know about the importance of teacher quality in particular, it is reasonable to surmise that lack of qualified teachers and adequate classroom space has the potential to seriously undermine any positive effects that might be expected to result from the investment in smaller class sizes (National Research Council 1999). Lack of an adequate infrastructure may compromise effectiveness and/or add substantially to the total price tag of the class size reduction policy. Further, on an equity note, wide-scale class size reduction policies like that in California can dramatically affect the distribution of teacher quality across communities. Care must be taken to ensure that schools with large concentrations of poor students do not end up with lower-quality teachers due to the limited supply of well-prepared new teachers coming into the system or the migration of their best teachers to more attractive school systems.

3.   *Context of policy and practice* — One study referred to class size reduction policies as an opportunity, not a treatment, implying that there are certain conditions under which reductions in class size can produce achievement gains (Anderson 2000). Two sorts of policy context issues are particularly relevant to this case. First, there is the notion of *complementary policies*, those that may increase the likelihood that class size reduction will have a positive effect. Teacher professional development is an example of a policy that may interact with class size reduction to yield a positive effect (Evertson 2000). Incentives for teachers to maximize the benefits of smaller classes are another. Second, there are *competing policies*, those that have the potential to be compromised in favor of class size reduction. Examples include alternative programs for at-risk students, higher teacher salaries, and extended school days. There is also the question of the classroom context. Some insights here are necessary to understand how and why class size reduction can work. We need a better sense of what teachers do in smaller classes that makes them more or less effective. Some research is occurring in this area (Betts and Shkolnik 1999; Brophy 2000; Rice 1999), and more is needed. The point is that the broader context of policy and practice can affect both the cost and the effectiveness of class size reduction.

4. Cost-benefit considerations — Reducing class sizes can be costly. Krueger's analysis suggests that small class sizes are cost-beneficial over the long term with respect to labor market outcomes. While some of the assumptions in that analysis can and should be challenged, the study represents a good starting point; this sort of work is necessary to inform decisions about whether small classes are worth the investment. However, there are lots of policy alternatives that may be found to be worth the investment, more than our limited stock of resources can support. The question is not simply, should we reduce class sizes, but rather, where are investments in education best made? Class size reduction is one possibility, but other popular alternatives include teacher salary increases, more time for instruction, and an expansion of early educational opportunities for youngsters. Each of these policy options could be shown to be worth the investment in a cost-benefit analysis. What is needed is a cost-effectiveness analysis to help guide perplexing decisions concerning *this* versus *that*. In addition, as indicated above, it may be a mistake to universally equate small with better. Rather, it might be wise to sort out the circumstances in which classes should be small and in which they can be large. Such research has the potential to result in policy decisions that are attractive from both cost and effectiveness perspectives.

Implications for research

In order to better understand the conditions under which investments in smaller classes make sense, future research should address four broad recommendations. First, there is a need for more meta-analyses that try to identify points of agreement among existing studies. This study will involve a more refined examination of the literature to identify patterns for specific types of students, subject areas, grade levels, and policy contexts. In other words, such analyses would work toward identifying the circumstances under which smaller class sizes are most effective.

Second, there is a need for improving the basic quality of new non-experimental studies conducted. Attention should focus on appropriate measures of key variables, model specification issues, and key assumptions underlying the studies. Including interactions with policy environment variables could help illuminate the conditions under which class size reduction works, and interactions with student background variables might shed light on who benefits most from investments in smaller classes.

Third, more experimentally designed studies could help bolster the confidence we have in the few that currently exist. The results from class size experiments are promising, but more work is needed to confirm what has been found thus far.

Finally, greater attention should be paid to estimating the costs of class size reduction and other alternatives so that researchers and policy makers can compare different policy options on cost-effectiveness grounds. Some progress has been made here by Krueger and others (see Brewer et al. 1999), but more work is needed — particularly studies that provide information on the economic trade-offs associated with alternative policy choices.

With ongoing attention to these sorts of issues, our understanding of this complex policy alternative will improve. As important is establishing a clear line of communication between the research and policy communities so that empirical findings about the impact of class size can be used to inform the policy-making process.

References

Anderson, L.W. 2000. "Why Should Reduced Class Size Lead to Reduced Student Achievement?" In M.C. Wang and J.D. Finn. eds., *How Small Classes Help Teachers Do Their Best*. Philadelphia, Pa.: Temple University Center for Research in Human Development and Education, pp. 3-24.

Angrist, Joshua, and Victor Lavy. 1999. "Using Maimonides' Rule to Estimate the Effect of Class Size on Children's Academic Achievement." *Quarterly Journal of Economics* 114(2): 533-75.

Bacolod, Marigee. 2001. "The Role of Alternative Opportunities in the Female Labor Market In Teacher Supply and Quality: 1940-1990." Los Angeles, Calif.: UCLA. Mimeo.

Betts, J.R., and J.L. Shkolnik. 1999. "The Behavioral Effects of Variations in Class Size: The Case of Math Teachers." *Educational Evaluation and Policy Analysis* 21(2): 193-214.

Betts, Julian R. 1996. "Is There a Link Between School Inputs and Earnings?" In Gary Burtless, ed., *Does Money Matter? The Effect of School Resources on Student Achievement and Adult Success*. Washington D.C.: Brookings Institution, pp. 141-91.

Bohrnstedt, G.W., B.M. Stecher, and E.W. Wiley. 2000. "The California Class Size Reduction Evaluation: Lessons Learned. In M.C. Wang and J.D. Finn. eds., *How Small Classes Help Teachers Do Their Best*. Philadelphia, Pa.: Temple University Center for Research in Human Development and Education, pp. 201-26.

Brewer, D., C. Krop, B.P. Gill, and R. Reichardt. 1999. "Estimating the Cost of National Class Size Reductions Under Different Policy Alternatives." *Educational Evaluation and Policy Analysis* 21(2): 179-92.

Brophy, J. 2000. "How Might Teachers Make Smaller Classes Better Classes? In M.C. Wang and J.D. Finn. eds., *How Small Classes Help Teachers Do Their Best*. Philadelphia, Pa.: Temple University Center for Research in Human Development and Education, pp. 35-64.

Brown, Charles, Curtis Gilroy, and Andrew Kohen. 1982. "The Effect of the Minimum Wage on Employment and Unemployment." *Journal of Economic Literature* 20 (June): 487-528.

Burkhead, Jesse. 1967. *Input-Output in Large City High Schools*. Syracuse, N.Y.: Syracuse University Press.

California Legislative Analyst's Office. 1997. *Policy Brief: Class Size Reduction*. Sacramento: California Legislative Analyst's Office.

Card, David. 1999. "The Causal Effect of Schooling on Earnings." In Orley Ashenfelter and David Card, eds., *Handbook of Labor Economics,* Amsterdam: North Holland. Forthcoming.

Card, David, and Alan B. Krueger. 1992a. "Does School Quality Matter? Returns to Education and the Characteristics of Public Schools in the United States." *Journal of Political Economy* 100(1): 1-40.

Card, David, and Alan B. Krueger. 1992b. "School Quality and Black-White Relative Earnings: A Direct Assessment." *Quarterly Journal of Economics* 107(1): 151-200.

Card, David, and Alan B. Krueger. 1995. *Myth and Measurement: The New Economics of the Minimum Wage.* Princeton, N.J.: Princeton University Press.

Card, David, and Alan B. Krueger. 1996. "Labor Market Effects of School Quality: Theory and Evidence." In Gary Burtless, ed., *Does Money Matter? The Effect of School Resources on Student Achievement and Adult Success.* Washington D.C.: Brookings Institution, pp. 97-140.

Card, David, and A. Abigail Payne. 1998. "School Finance Reform, the Distribution of School Spending, and the Distribution of SAT Scores." *Journal of Public Economics,* forthcoming.

Cawley, John, Karen Conneely, James Heckman, and Edward Vytlacil. 1996. "Measuring the Effects of Cognitive Ability." Working Paper No. 5645. Cambridge, Mass.: National Bureau of Economic Research.

Chubb, John E., and Terry M. Moe. 1990. *Politics, Markets and America's Schools.* Washington, D.C.: Brookings Institution.

Clune, W.H. 1994. "Equity and Adequacy in Education: Issues for Policy and Finance." *Educational Policy* 8(4).

Cohn, E., and S.D. Millman. 1975. *Input-Output Analysis in Public Education.* Cambridge, Mass.: Ballinger.

Coleman, James S., Ernest Q. Campbell, Carol J. Hobson, James McPartland, Alexander M. Mood, Frederic D. Weinfeld, and Robert L. York. 1966. *Equality of Educational Opportunity.* Washington, D.C.: U.S. Government Printing Office.

Congressional Budget Office. 1986. *Trends in Educational Achievement.* Washington, D.C.: Congressional Budget Office.

Currie, Janet, and Duncan Thomas. 1999. "Early Test Scores, Socioeconomic Status, and Future Outcomes." Working Paper No. 6943. Cambridge, Mass.: National Bureau of Economic Research.

Currie, Janet, and Duncan Thomas. 2000. "Early Test Scores, Socioeconomic Status, School Quality, and Future Outcomes." Department of Economics, UCLA (mimeo).

Ellison, Glenn. 2000. "Evolving Standards for Academic Publishing: A q-r Theory." Cambridge, Mass.: MIT. Mimeo.

Evertson, C.M. 2000. "Professional Development and Implementation of Class Size Reduction." In M.C. Wang and J.D. Finn. eds., *How Small Classes Help Teachers Do Their Best.* Philadelphia, Pa.: Temple University Center for Research in Human Development and Education, pp. 25-34.

Finn, Chester E. 1991. *We Must Take Charge,* New York: Free Press.

Finn, Jeremy D., and Charles M. Achilles. 1990. "Answers and Questions about Class Size: A Statewide Experiment." *American Educational Research Journal* 27(3): 557-77.

Finn, Jeremy D., and Charles M. Achilles. 1999. "Tennessee's Class Size Study: Findings, Implications, and Misconceptions." *Educational Evaluation and Policy Analysis* 21(2): 97-110.

Folger, John, and Jim Parker. 1990. "The Cost-Effectiveness of Adding Aides or Reducing Class Size." Vanderbilt University, mimeo.

Fowler, W., and H. Walberg. 1991. "School Size, Characteristics, and Outcomes." *Educational Evaluation and Policy Analysis* 13(2): 189-202.

Galbraith, John Kenneth. 1955. *Economics and the Art of Controversy.* New York: Vintage Books.

Grissmer, David W. 1999. "Class Size Effects: Assessing the Evidence, Its Policy Implications, and Future Research Agenda. *Educational Evaluation and Policy Analysis* 21(2): 231-48.

Grissmer, David W. 2001. *Improving Student Achievement: What State NAEP Test Scores Tell Us.* Washington, D.C.: Rand Institute.

Grissmer, David W., Sheila Nataraj Kirby, Mark Berends, and Stephanie Williamson. 1994. *Student Achievement and the Changing American Family.* Santa Monica, Calif.: Rand Corporation.

Hanushek, Eric A. 1981. "Throwing Money at Schools." *Journal of Policy Analysis and Management* 1(1): 19-41.

Hanushek, Eric A. 1986. "The Economics of Schooling: Production and Efficiency in Public Schools." *Journal of Economic Literature* 24(3): 1141-77.

Hanushek, Eric A. 1989. "Expenditures, Efficiency, and Equity in Education: The Federal Government's Role." *American Economic Review* 79(2): 46-51.

Hanushek, Eric A. 1992. "The Trade-Off Between Child Quantity and Quality." *Journal of Political Economy* 100(1): 84-117.

Hanushek, Eric A. 1996a. "A More Complete Picture of School Resource Policies." *Review of Educational Research* 66: 397-409.

Hanushek, Eric A. 1996b. "School Resources and Student Performance." In Gary Burtless, ed., *Does Money Matter? The Effect of School Resources on Student Achievement and Adult Success.* Washington D.C.: Brookings Institution, pp. 43-73.

Hanushek, Eric A. 1997. "Assessing the Effects of School Resources on Student Performance: An Update." *Educational Evaluation and Policy Analysis* 19(2): 141-64.

Hanushek, Eric A. 1998a. "Conclusions and Controversies about the Effectiveness of School Resources." *FRBNY Economic Policy Review* 4 (March): 11-28.

Hanushek, Eric A. 1998b. "The Evidence on Class Size." Occasional Paper Number 98-1. Rochester, N.Y.: W. Allen Wallis Institute of Political Economy, University of Rochester.

Hanushek, Eric A. 1999a. "The Evidence on Class Size." In Susan E. Mayer and Paul Peterson, eds., *Earning and Learning: How Schools Matter.* Washington, D.C.: Brookings Institution.

Hanushek, Eric A. 1999b. "Some Findings From an Independent Investigation of the Tennessee STAR Experiment and From Other Investigations of Class Size Effects." *Educational Evaluation and Policy Analysis* 21(2): 143-63.

Hanushek, Eric A. 2001. "Black-White Achievement Differences and Governmental Interventions." *American Economic Review* 91(2).

Hanushek, Eric A., and Steven G. Rivkin. 1997. "Understanding the Twentieth-Century Growth in U.S. School Spending." *Journal of Human Resources* 32(1): 35-68.

Hanushek, Eric A., et al. 1994. *Making Schools Work: Improving Performance and Controlling Costs.* Washington, D.C.: Brookings Institution.

Hanushek, Eric A., Steven G. Rivkin, and Lori L. Taylor. 1996. "Aggregation and the Estimated Effects of School Resources." *Review of Economics and Statistics* 78(4): 611-27.

Harnisch, Delwyn L. 1987. "Characteristics Associated With Effective Public High Schools." *Journal of Educational Research* 80(4): 233-41.

Harris, D. 2002. "Optimal School and Teacher Inputs." In Henry Levin and Patrick McKewan, eds., *American Education Finance Association 2002 Yearbook.* Washington, D.C.: American Education Finance Association. Forthcoming.

Heckman, James S., Anne Layne-Farrar, and Petra Todd. 1996a. "Does Measured School Quality Really Matter? An Examination of the Earnings-Quality Relationship." In Gary Burtless, ed., *Does Money Matter? The Effect of School Resources on Student Achievement and Adult Success.* Washington, D.C.: Brookings Institution.

Heckman, James, Anne Layne-Farrar, and Petra Todd. 1996b. "Human Capital Pricing Equations With an Application to Estimating the Effect of Schooling Quality on Earnings." *Review of Economics and Statistics* 78(4): 562-610.

Hedges, L.V., R.D. Laine, and R. Greenwald. 1994. "Does Money Matter? A Meta-Analysis of Studies of the Effects of Differential School Inputs on Student Outcomes. *Educational Researcher* 23(3): 5-14.

Hedges, Larry V. 1990. "Directions for Future Methodology." In Kenneth W. Wachter and Miron L. Straf, eds., *The Future of Meta-Analysis.* New York, N.Y.: Russell Sage.

Hedges, Larry V., and Ingram Olkin. 1985. *Statistical Methods for Meta-Analysis.* Orlando, Fla.: Academic Press.

Hedges, Larry V., Richard Laine, and Rob Greenwald. 1994. "Does Money Matter? A Meta- Analysis of Studies of the Effects of Differential School Inputs on Student Outcomes." *Education Researcher* 23(3): 5-14.

Heim, John, and Lewis Perl. 1974. *The Educational Production Function: Implications for Educational Manpower Policy.* Institute of Public Employment. Monograph No. 4. Ithaca, N.Y.: Cornell University.

Jencks, Christopher S., and M. Brown. 1975. "Effects of High Schools on their Students." *Harvard Educational Review* 45(3): 273-324.

Jencks, Christopher S., and Meredith Phillips. 1999. "Aptitude or Achievement: Why Do Test Scores Predict Educational Attainment and Earnings?" In Susan Mayer and Paul Peterson, eds., *Learning and Earning: How Schools Matter.* Washington, D.C.: Brookings Institution Press. Forthcoming.

Kiesling, Herbert. 1965. "Measuring a Local Government Service: A Study of School Districts in New York State." Ph.D. Dissertation, Harvard University, Cambridge, Mass.

Kiesling, Herbert. 1967. "Measuring a Local Government Service: A Study of School Districts in New York State." *Review of Economics and Statistics* 49 (August): 356-67.

Kiesling, Herbert. 1984. "Assignment Practices and the Relationship of Instructional Time to the Reading Performance of Elementary School Children." *Economics of Education Review* 3(4): 341-50.

Krueger, Alan B. 1999. "Experimental Estimates of Education Production Functions." *Quarterly Journal of Economics* 114(2): 497-532.

Krueger, Alan B. 1999a. "Measuring Labor's Share." *American Economic Review* 89(2): 45-51.

Krueger, Alan B. 1999b. "Experimental Estimates of Educational Production Functions." *Quarterly Journal of Economics* 114(2): 497-532.

Krueger, Alan B., and Diane Whitmore. 1999. "The Effect of Attending a Small Class in the Early Grades on College-Test Taking and Middle School Test Results: Evidence From Project STAR." Working Paper No. 427. Princeton, N.J.: Princeton Industrial Relations Section.

Laine, R.D., R. Greenwald, and L.V. Hedges. 1996. "Money Does Matter: A Research Synthesis of a New Universe of Education Production Function Studies." In L.O. Picus and J.L. Wattenbarger, eds., *Where Does the Money Go? Resource Allocation in Elementary and Secondary Schools*. Thousand Oaks, Calif.: Corwin, pp. 44-70.

Lakdawalla, Darius. 2001. "The Declining Quality of Teachers." Working Paper No. 8263. Cambridge, Mass.: National Bureau of Economic Research.

Lazear, Edward. 1999. "Educational Production." Working Paper No. 7349. Cambridge, Mass.: National Bureau of Economic Research.

Lazear, Edward. 2000. "Educational Production." *Quarterly Journal of Economics*. Forthcoming.

Lewit, Eugene M., and Linda Schuurmann Baker. 1997. "Class Size." *The Future of Children* 7(3): 112-21.

Lindahl, Mikael. 2000. "Home Versus Summer Learning: A New Approach to Estimating the Effect of Class Size on Achievement." Stockholm University. Mimeo.

Link, Charles R., and James G. Mulligan. 1986. "The Merits of a Longer School Day." *Economics of Education Review* 5(4): 373-81.

Link, Charles R., and James G. Mulligan. 1991. "Classmates' Effects on Black Student Achievement in Public School Classrooms." *Economics of Education Review* 10(4): 297-310.

Maynard, Rebecca, and D. Crawford. 1976. "School Performance." *Rural Income Maintenance Experiment: Final Report*. Madison: University of Wisconsin.

Molnar, A., P. Smith, J. Zahorki, A. Palmer, A. Halbach, and K. Ehrle. 1999. "Evaluating the SAGE Program: A Pilot Program in Targeted Pupil-Teacher Reduction in Wisconsin." *Educational Evaluation and Policy Analysis* 21(2): 165-78.

Montmarquette, Claude, and Sophie Mahseredjian. 1989. "Does School Matter for Educational Achievement? A Two-Way Nested-Error Components Analysis." *Journal of Applied Econometrics* 4: 181-93.

Mosteller, Frederick. 1995. "The Tennessee Study of Class Size in the Early School Grades." *The Future of Children* 5(2): 113-27.

Murnane, Richard, John Willet, and Frank Levy. 1995. "The Growing Importance of Cognitive Skills in Wage Determination." *Review of Economics and Statistics* 77: 251-66.

National Research Council. 1999. *Making Money Matter: Financing America's Schools*. Washington, D.C.: National Academy Press.

Neal, Derek, and William Johnson. 1996. "The Role of Premarket Factors in Black-White Wage Differentials." *Journal of Political Economy* 104 (October): 869-95.

Nye, B., L.V. Hedges, and S. Konstantopoulos. 1999. "The Long-Term Effects of Small Classes: A Five-Year Follow-up of the Tennessee Class Size Experiment." *Educational Evaluation and Policy Analysis* 21(2): 127-42.

Nye, Barbara, Jayne Zaharias, B.D. Fulton, et al. 1994. "The Lasting Benefits Study: A Continuing Analysis of the Effect of Small Class Size in Kindergarten Through Third Grade on Student Achievement Test Scores in Subsequent Grade Levels." Seventh grade technical report. Nashville: Center of Excellence for Research in Basic Skills, Tennessee State University.

Rice, J.K. 1999. "The Impact of Class Size on Instructional Strategies and the Use of Time in High School Mathematics and Science Courses." *Educational Evaluation and Policy Analysis* 21(2): 215-30.

Rivkin, Steven G., Eric A. Hanushek, and John F. Kain. 2000. "Teachers, Schools, and Academic Achievement." Working Paper No. 6691 (revised). Cambridge, Mass: National Bureau of Economic Research.

Sanders, William L., and Sandra P. Horn. 1995. "The Tennessee Value-Added Assessment System (TVAA): Mixed Model Methodology in Educational Assessement." In Anthony J. Shinkfield and Daniel L. Stufflebeam, eds., *Teacher Evaluation: Guide to Effective Practice*. Boston, Mass.: Kluwer Academic Publishers.

Sengupta, J.K., and Sfeir, R.E. 1986. "Production Frontier Estimates of Scale in Public Schools in California." *Economics of Education Review* 5(3): 297-307.

Smith, Marshall. 1972. "*Equality of Educational Opportunity*: The Basic Findings Reconsidered." In Frederick Mosteller and Daniel P. Moynihan, eds., *On Equality of Educational Opportunity*. New York, N.Y.: Random House, pp. 230-342.

Speakman, Robert, and Finis Welch. 1995. "Does School Quality Matter? A Reassessment." Texas A&M University. Mimeo.

Stanley, T.D. 2001. "Wheat From Chaff: Meta-Analysis as Quantitative Literature Review." *Journal of Economic Perspectives*, forthcoming.

Stecher, Brian M., and George W. Bohrnstedt, eds. 1999. *Class Size Reduction in California: Early Evaluation Findings, 1996-98.* Palo Alto, Calif: American Institutes for Research.

Stecher, B. M. and G. W. Bohrnstedt. 2000. *Class size reduction in California: The 1998-99 Evaluation Findings.* Sacramento, CA: California Department of Education, August.

Stern, D. 1989. "Educational Cost Factors and Student Achievement in Grades 3 and 6: Some New Evidence." *Economics of Education Review* 8(2): 149-58.

Summers, Anita, and Barbara Wolfe. 1977. "Do Schools Make a Difference?" *American Economic Review* 67(4): 649-52.

Wenglinsky, Harold. 1997. *When Money Matters.* Princeton, N.J.: Policy Information Center, Educational Testing Service.

Word, Elizabeth, John Johnston, Helen Pate Bain, B. DeWayne Fulton, Jayne Boyd Zaharies, Martha Nannette Lintz, Charles M. Achilles, John Folger, and Carolyn Breda. 1990. *Student/Teacher Achievement Ratio (STAR), Tennessee's K-3 Class Size Study: Final Summary Report, 1985-1990.* Nashville: Tennessee State Department of Education.

About EPI

The Economic Policy Institute was founded in 1986 to widen the debate about policies to achieve healthy economic growth, prosperity, and opportunity.

Today, despite recent rapid growth in the U.S. economy, inequality in wealth, wages, and income remains historically high. Expanding global competition, changes in the nature of work, and rapid technological advances are altering economic reality. Yet many of our policies, attitudes, and institutions are based on assumptions that no longer reflect real world conditions.

With the support of leaders from labor, business, and the foundation world, the Institute has sponsored research and public discussion of a wide variety of topics: trade and fiscal policies; trends in wages, incomes, and prices; education; the causes of the productivity slowdown; labor market problems; rural and urban policies; inflation; state-level economic development strategies; comparative international economic performance; and studies of the overall health of the U.S. manufacturing sector and of specific key industries.

The Institute works with a growing network of innovative economists and other social science researchers in universities and research centers all over the country who are willing to go beyond the conventional wisdom in considering strategies for public policy.

Founding scholars of the Institute include Jeff Faux, EPI president; Lester Thurow, Sloan School of Management, MIT; Ray Marshall, former U.S. secretary of labor, professor at the LBJ School of Public Affairs, University of Texas; Barry Bluestone, University of Massachusetts-Boston; Robert Reich, former U.S. secretary of labor; and Robert Kuttner, author, editor of *The American Prospect,* and columnist for *Business Week* and the Washington Post Writers Group.

For additional information about the Institute, contact EPI at 1660 L Street NW, Suite 1200, Washington, DC 20036, (202) 775-8810, or visit www.epinet.org.